race
and
races

race
and
races

SECOND EDITION

Richard A. Goldsby
UNIVERSITY OF MARYLAND

Macmillan Publishing Co., Inc.
NEW YORK

Collier Macmillan Publishers
LONDON

Macmillan Publishing Co., Inc.
866 Third Avenue, New York, New York 10022

Collier Macmillan Canada, Ltd.

Library of Congress Cataloging in Publication Data

Goldsby, Richard A
  Race and races.

  Includes bibliographies and index.
  1. Race. I. Title.
GN269.G64   1976   572   76-1903
ISBN 0-02-344310-3

Printing: 1 2 3 4 5 6 7 8   Year: 7 8 9 0 1 2 3

To
John,
Elizabeth,
Joanna,
and
Marilyn

foreword

Race is a biological phenomenon, racism a sociological attitude. Because racism has led to wholesale misery and crime, the existence of races has often been denied. The author of this book, *Race and Races,* begins with an acknowledgment of the biological situation that mankind falls into a diversity of populations, which are called races. He is aware from facts known about dogs, sparrows, and flies that races, including those of men, are distinguished by different frequencies of genes; that the genic content of any one race includes a great array of different genetic constitutions; that there are no "pure" races; that the diversity of constitutions of different races overlaps greatly; and that—for all these reasons—a racial population and the individuals belonging to it are two very different entities, the populations being a complex pool of genes, and the individuals representing unique samples from this pool.

The silent or openly expressed assumption that races can be graded along a scale from inferior to superior has been made by peoples and tribes all over the globe since the dawn of history. It has left all of us with scars and prejudging inclinations. Dr. Goldsby has tried hard and successfully to control prejudice by giving a fair account of the problems presented by the existence of races. His book is that of a man who knows his subject as a scientist and who also perceives the social meaning of his findings and interpretations. His book will clarify the issue of race for many who may come to it with vague popular notions of various shades and of opposite viewpoints. Nevertheless, the author permits the reader to judge on his own, although he does not hide his personal accent. It is a good sign in our troubled times that such a book has been written. It will do its part in our endeavors to make the future a better one.

Curt Stern

Berkeley, California

preface

n 1969 the *Harvard Educational Review* published an article by Arthur Jensen entitled "How Much Can We Boost IQ and Scholastic Achievement?" In this article Jensen questioned and laid siege to the central assumption of compensatory education: the idea that all groups possess equal inherent intellectual potential and, therefore, any differences in achievement observed when one group is compared with another must be a consequence of differences in the environments each has experienced. In an attack that began with his now widely quoted slogan, "compensatory education has been tried and apparently failed," Jensen questioned the assumption of an equal distribution of innate potential among racial groups. In particular, he suggested that the differences seen in the academic achievements of Blacks and Whites reflect an innate, that is to say, genetic, difference in the intellectual potentials of these groups. More than any other article, "How Much Can We Boost IQ and Scholastic Achievement?" has been responsible for the renewed interest in the meaning and significance of race.

It was after reading the Jensen paper in 1969 that I prepared the first edition of *Race and Races* in order to provide a basic introduction to the biological reality, meaning, and limited significance of race. During the years since the preparation of that first edition, new information and new points of view have developed. Some of these are sufficiently important to make even so basic a primer as *Race and Races* incomplete and distorted without their inclusion. Furthermore, as this latest episode in the race–mental ability argument continues,[1] I find it increasingly difficult to affect in my writing

---

[1] The debate over the equal distribution of intellectual potential is a recurrent theme in American political history. In the 1920's laws were passed designed to slow the flood of Jewish and Eastern European immigrants into the United States to a trickle. The legislators used as a justification specious assertations that these peoples were intellectually inferior. And, before the 1920's, during the antebellum 1800's, arguments for maintaining slavery included questionable "proofs" of Black inferiority.

a neutrality which belies my enlistment—by birth and conviction—against the views expressed by Professor Jensen. Consequently, this second edition is a bit more contentious than its predecessor. It is also more robust as a result of the inclusion of new material on race and mental ability, milk intolerance, the inheritance of skin color, and quantitative comparisons of the genetic diversity both within and between races.

My thanks go out to those colleagues who have encouraged me in the preparation of this second edition of *Race and Races*. Their suggestions have been extremely valuable in shaping the direction of this revision. I am also much indebted to Mrs. Margaret Schaffer who carefully prepared and diligently guarded the grammatical integrity of the manuscript. And, finally, I want to acknowledge that it is always a pleasure to prepare a book with the editorial, art, and production departments of Macmillan.

Richard A. Goldsby

Palo Alto, California

contents

race
and
races

1
a synopsis

No, Mr. Vonnegut, they are not still teaching that. At least not all of them are. Diversity, not uniformity, is the rule in nature, and the varieties of men we recognize as races are an expression of that pattern of diversity. The existence of human races and their intrinsic differences are facts which can be documented. Characteristic racial differences can be demonstrated for indicators as diverse as blood type, fingerprint pattern, and in some cases even composition of the urine. For instance, if we had three groups of people, say a group of Whites from northern Europe, several Japanese, and a number of Blacks, we could distinguish these racial groups from each other without ever looking at them. We could do so on the basis of known average racial differences in fingerprint pattern (Mongoloids have more whorls than Whites or Blacks); blood types (Whites have more Rh negatives than either Blacks or Mongoloids); and urine (the Japanese population will be distinctive in containing a large number of individuals who excrete a particular amino acid). We could even identify the Japanese on the basis of their ear wax. Most of them have a dry, crumbly type of ear wax whereas that of most Blacks and Caucasoids is more sticky and adhesive. It is clear that there are profound constitutional differences between racial populations. Everybody isn't just like everybody else.

Because misconception and misunderstanding of the significance of racial differences carry such great potential for harm, it is important to display and interpret the known facts about constitutional racial differences correctly and to place observations of racial differences in proper social perspective. The lessons of history illustrate the dangers that lie in an incorrect interpretation of the nature, meaning, and significance of race. Incorrect interpretation has been responsible for most tragic examples of systematic inhumanity and gratuitous intergroup violence. Just a little more than 35 years ago, offering specious arguments of Nordic racial superiority as a justification for its horrors, Nazi racism exterminated whole peoples. The incorrect and finally illegitimate doctrine of White superiority with its corollary of Black inferiority runs like an ugly thread through the entire fabric of American history. The crucial factor responsible for the introduction of such dangerous racist aberrations into the pattern of societies is the step from the recognition of palpable racial differences to an assumption of racial superiority. In the recent history of the world some racial groups have been too ready to believe that the lower technological accomplishments of other races were inherent and genetically determined rather than a reflection of life styles and the vagaries of history. This assumption of a constitutional inferiority provided the fundamental justification for the appropriation of the land of the North American Indians, the treasure of the Aztecs, and the very bodies of Blacks.

Against such a background of recorded past and possible future episodes of racially inspired malevolence it is understandable that some who are interested in bettering race relations seek to do so by denying the existence of human races. If one can prove there are no races of man, then, logically, racial bigotry and the evil resulting from its practice can be eliminated. Those who feel that the concept of race, no matter how carefully formulated, is a myth hold that supposed biological differences between races of man are, in an absolute sense, without biological reality or meaning. In popular extension, this point of view holds that apparent racial differences are superficial, only skin deep, and that men are really brothers under the skin.

From what has gone before it should be clear that this will not be the conclusion reached by this book. It is true that all men are related by their common humanity and by the common capacities that human potential confers on them, but when a six-foot Swede and a five-foot Pygmy shake hands, they are not mistaken for brothers, no matter how amicable and warm their meeting. Tall men and short men, Jews and Gentiles, for that matter men and women live in harmony not because they are alike, but because they try to respect, admire, trust, understand, and even love each other. I do not believe it is useful or even desirable to try to promote harmony between races by denying that there are biological differences between them. Acceptance of the differences, together with an appreciation of their significance, is a more secure foundation on which to build racial harmony.

What Is a Race?

A race is a breeding population. A breeding population is one which for reasons of geography or culture mates largely within itself. As examples of breeding populations that we can call races we can include groups such as the Australian Aborigine and the American Black. On the other hand, it is inaccurate to speak of groups such as the Jews, who share much common culture but not a common pool of inheritance, as a race. The Australian Aborigines exist as a race primarily because of geographical factors. The isolation of their homeland, the island-continent of Australia, has for millenia insured that mating will take place with fellow islanders. The American Black is a relatively new and hybrid race maintained as a breeding population by social factors. Segregation and custom rather than geography make it likely that the majority (though the rainbow-like diversity of this group makes it clear that by no means all) of matings will be with other American Blacks. Jews, on the other hand, though a closely knit cultural group, are not a race because they are not a single but rather many different breeding populations. Two thousand years ago, in the Diaspora, the Jewish people were deliberately scattered by the Romans. In spite of the dispersion, Jews have managed to maintain their faith and have often adopted highly parallel cultural solutions to the problems they encountered as minorities. However, the racial makeup of these various Jewish populations changed, more and more diverging from each other and in most cases coming to resemble that of the people among whom they settled. The lack of racial identity of Jews is best illustrated by the diversity found in the Jewish state of Israel. There one sees a culture made up of a racial spectrum ranging from whites of northern Europe to browns from Africa and the Near East.

Members of the same race have more of their hereditary components in common with each other than with members of different breeding populations. This does not mean that all members of the same race are alike. There is enormous diversity within as well as between racial groups. It is not as though each race came from a single Adam and Eve, with every member of the race tracing his ancestry back to that pair of very great grandparents. The ancestry of all races is to some degree mixed, as though every race has had not one but multiple Adams and Eves. In most cases, too, there have been interracial matings which have from time to time introduced new and different sources of inheritance. Members of a particular race differ so much from each other because they are each the offspring of different parents each of whom traces a different lineage containing differing contributions from other breeding populations. Races are much more like stews than homogenized sauces.

Because of the diversity within races, the concept of race has most meaning when applied to populations rather than to individuals. Imagine how little meaning it would have in terms of the over-all nature of a Mulligan stew to describe or specify in great detail the composition of a single potato or chunk of meat in the stew. Similarly one does not learn much about the nature of a race by studying a single member of the race. What one is interested in is the over-all composition—the entire recipe. We have already seen that it is possible to establish statistical criteria for recognizing racial populations. For instance, when one encounters a population in which the majority of individuals have type O, Rh positive blood, dry ear wax, and a characteristic fingerprint pattern, he can identify that population as American Indian. Paradoxically, though, if he were asked to predict the fingerprint pattern or the blood type of any particular Indian in that same population, he could not do so with certainty. If, for example, a doctor assumed, without checking, that every pint of blood from an Indian reservation was type O he would not only be incorrect but criminally negligent. It is crucial to bear in mind that racial characterizations reflect the average for a group but cannot describe the isolated individual, who is unique.

Some students of race have suggested that all of the races we see in the world today arose by combinations of a few—maybe four or five—basic racial types. This theory may or may not be true. We do not know enough about the origin of human races to say. What we can say is that there are far more than four or five major breeding populations of mankind today. Actually, even by conservative estimation, more than two dozen breeding populations and hence races can be recognized. This list includes such diverse groups as the American Indian, the Northwest European, the Southeast Asian, the Bushman, the Mediterranean peoples, the West African Black, the Australian Aborigine, and the American Black.

As we have seen, the concept of race has most biological meaning when it is applied to populations, rather than to individuals. However, there have been many attempts to define race in individual terms, most of them juridical systems of racial classification that have been established more with an eye to politics and social custom than biological reality. Consider the description of one's racial identity as a Jew contained in the anti-Semitic Nurnberg laws of Nazi Germany.

In the first regulation of the Reich Citizenship Law, membership in the Jewish ''race'' is defined:

A Jew is anyone who descended from at least three grandparents who were racially fully Jews. A Jew is also one who descended from two full Jewish parents if (a) he belonged to the Jewish religious community at the time this law was issued or he joined the community later; (b) he was married to a Jewish person at the time this law was issued or married one subsequently; (c) he is the offspring from marriage with a Jew contracted after the law for the protection of German Blood and German Honor became effective; (d) he is the offspring of an extramarital relationship with a Jew and was born out of wedlock.

In the Law for the Protection of German Blood and German Honor we see some of the consequences that flow from these absurd and biologically meaningless definitions of the Jewish "race." This second of the Nürnberg race laws decreed the following:

Permeated by the knowledge that the purity of the German blood is the basis for the permanence of the German people and animated by the inflexible determination to safeguard the German nation for all time, the Reichstag has unanimously decreed the following law:

1. Marriages between Jews and citizens of German or similar blood are forbidden.
2. Extramarital intercourse between Jews and citizens of German and similar blood is forbidden.
3. Jews may not employ female citizens of German and similar blood under forty-five years of age in their households.

Germany enacted the laws which contained these peculiar definitions of a nonexistent race during the 1930's in an orgy of hysteria. Wild schemes for the protection of "German blood" from Jewish "pollution" were common. One of the most bizarre of these involved using a pendulum as a sort of divining rod to detect individuals with "Jewish" blood.

Some may be surprised to learn that laws aimed at protecting imagined "racial purity" have not been the exclusive property of Nazism. Until the Supreme Court ruled them unconstitutional in 1966, miscegenation laws designed to protect the "purity" of the White race were part of the legal codes of many states in this country. Here are some examples of statutes containing legal definitions of one's identity as a Negro:

1. A miscegenation statute of Missouri decreed it was a felony for Whites to marry Negroes. "Negroes are defined as persons having one-eighth part or more of Negro blood."
2. An Arkansas statute stated that it was a misdemeanor for any White person to marry "any person who has in her or his veins any Negro blood whatsoever."
3. A Texas miscegenation law stated that it was a felony for Whites to marry "Africans or descendants of Africans."

All of these legal definitions of race, whether based on religious and cultural associations or on naive considerations of geographical origins or blood fractions, are of little use in establishing a biolog-ically meaningful definition of race. This biological irrelevance is not surprising, however; legal definitions of race are designed not to serve scientific rationality but rather to lay the groundwork for the persecution or exclusion of individuals. Specifically, the Nürn-berg Race Laws were concocted to assure the removal of Jews (an ancient and distinguished people but hardly a race) from participa-tion in German life. Here in the United States miscegenation codes were part of a pattern of discriminatory laws designed to keep the Black population socially as well as sexually isolated from Whites. In short, legal definitions of race usually reflect prevailing ideas of racial superiority and purity rather than considerations of demon-strated biological fact.

Why Discuss Race?

We do not discuss race merely to recognize and point out varia-tions between groups. We want to see what contributions an ex-ploration of the biology of race can make to a discussion of two larger questions, one of considerable academic interest, the other of great practical importance. First, for the satisfaction of our own curiosity we want to know why there are different races and how they might have come to be. Second, given the observed biolog-ical differences among races what, if any, is their significance for society?

In order to answer the question of racial origins it is necessary to look into the origin of man himself and consider how biological variation may have played a role in his successful adaptation to many different environments. During the course of his evolution, we know that man, like all other living things, responded to his environment by adapting biologically. Many of the characteristics such as skin color and body build that we recognize as associated with race, represent adaptations evolved by man living in widely differing environments. Since his emergence in the warm, sunny climates of Africa some two million years ago man has successfully invaded and made his home in vastly different areas of the world. A key to man's global success has been the ability of different human populations to evolve variations in skin color, body struc-ture, blood chemistry, and physiology best suited for survival in different environments.

The differences in skin color we see in various human popula-tions probably arose in response to differing intensities of sunlight striking the parts of the globe that those various populations called home. Solar intensity is highest in the tropics and least in the extreme southern and northern latitudes. If we look at the distribution of skin color among human populations prior to 1492 and the voyages of discovery, we encounter progressively darker skins as we approach the tropics. Penetration of the skin by sunlight causes the production of vitamin D in a layer of tissue just under the skin. If this layer receives insufficient sunlight, too little vitamin D is produced. Vitamin D deficiency causes the softening of the bones assocated with rickets. Too much vitamin D results in excessive calcium uptake and deposition; bones become brittle and easily broken and calcium deposited in the kidneys produces stones. In the early days of man's existence he did not have such cultural adaptations as vitamin-D-enriched milk and sun-shielding pith helmets to compensate for too little or too much sun. Consequently early man's skin was the filter that regulated his absorption of sunlight. In the northerly climes, there was a genetic selection favoring fair skins that efficiently passed the faint rays of the cool north sun. Around the tropics selective pressures favored a heavily pigmented skin that dramatically reduced the amount of sun penetrating to the vitamin D synthesis layer. So when we look at the tropical populations of Asia and Africa, at peoples who have inhabited this sun-belt for millennia, we are not surprised to find the black skins of Africa, the browns of southern Asia, and the blacks of southern India and Ceylon.

Some of the differences in body build that we see between racial populations probably also arose as adaptations to climates. Contrast the long-limbed, slim bodies of some African Black populations with the short-limbed, generously fleshed body type found in populations of Greenland Eskimos. Both are body types well suited to the environments where they are found. Cold climates favor a heavy, heat-conserving body with short extremities. A hot climate favors a relatively lean body with long extremities. Such a body type has a high surface-to-volume ratio that exchanges heat with the environment. Careful studies which effectively measure surface-to-volume ratio show that populations in hot climates do indeed tend to have larger numbers of individuals with heat-dissipating high surface-to-volume ratios than those in colder climates such as that of Europe.

I do not mean to suggest that every racial characteristic is or has been a significant factor in the survival of the population that it marks. The survival value of appropriate skin color or body build is clear, but what about a "shoveled" incisor or a blue penis? Shoveling of the incisors, a condition in which the inner surfaces of the incisors are concave, is common in Mongoloid populations.

Some populations of South American Indians display a high frequency of blue penises. In considering the origin of races, we find that a number of such "passenger" traits (nonpaying in a survival sense but along for the ride) have been included in the inheritance of racial populations. Such variations are due to two factors — the vagaries of chance and racial interbreeding. Both chance and interbreeding introduce characteristics into populations which though fascinating to those who find it amusing to classify races have no role in aiding or hindering survival.

Allowing that human races exist it is clear that they must have originated. It is also clear that their origins are accomplished, even if poorly understood, matters of fact, finished and behind us. What can an inquiry into the matter of race contribute to an understanding of ourselves and our fellow men in other racial groups? What are the social implications of race? Exploring this question on which nearly everyone has an opinion we must recognize that there are extreme positions. At one extreme is the conviction that race is of primary and critical importance in determining the ability of an individual to function in a particular society. At the other end of the spectrum is the assertion that the notion of race is a fundamentally useless and impractical one. Recognizing that one of these positions, the one that suggests much of an individual's behavior rests on a racial foundation, is more socially dangerous than the other, both are incorrect.

As emphasized earlier, the notion of race is statistical and describes the characteristics of populations. It does not and cannot describe a particular individual in a population. Any attempt to predict the intelligence, the body build, the blood type, or even the skin color of an individual from a knowledge of his racial population is hopeless. All Northwest Europeans are not fair-skinned, all Blacks are not black, and all Japanese are not short-statured. Given the internal variation of races, it is obvious that the general characteristics of the populations tell little about the specifics of an individual in that population.

At the same time, there are implications of practical importance that flow from the notion of race. For instance, race has important medical implications. A number of diseases are race-related. Two good examples are sickle-cell anemia and Tay-Sachs disease.

In the United States sickle-cell anemia is found almost exclusively among Blacks. This hereditary disease is characterized by a failure of the red blood cells to carry sufficient oxygen and their assumption of a sicklelike shape. The particular gene for sickle-cell anemia may be carried in a recessive or silent state by individuals who are healthy themselves. The existence of healthy carriers is accounted for by the fact that, with few exceptions, an individual carries two sets of each hereditary determinant or gene. One set comes from the father and the other from the mother. If a person carries one sickling gene but also a normal gene for the characteristic, the normal gene will be dominant. However, when two healthy carriers mate and produce offspring there is a 25 per cent chance that a child produced by their union will receive a sickling gene from each parent. When an individual bears two sickling genes the debilitating and often fatal disease of sickle-cell anemia results.

In some American Black populations as many as one person in ten is a healthy carrier of the sickling gene. As long as these individuals do not mate with other carriers there is no danger of producing sickle-celled offspring. However, marriages between carriers suffer a heavy liability imposed by the 25 per cent chance of producing offspring with sickle-cell anemia. The implications of such a situation for medicine are clear. The physician practicing pediatrics must be alerted for the occurrence of this malady among his young Black patients. However, the implications of this race-related phenomenon extend beyond the practice of the individual physician and into the realm of preventive public health. It is possible to perform a relatively simple blood analysis that will detect the healthy carriers of the sickling gene. And since in many states it is necessary to take a blood test for syphilis before a marriage license is issued, further tests of the blood would allow one to determine if both partners are healthy carriers of the sickling trait. If so, they could be allowed to marry but told of the dangers of their mating and advised to adopt children. It is a personal tragedy for many families and suffering children that this clear and needed step to reduce the incidence of sickle-cell anemia has not been taken by the public health agencies of the several states.

Tay-Sachs disease (TSD) is a hereditary disease that results in the progressive deterioration of the brain. Afflicted individuals usually die within two years of birth. It is found in populations of Jews who happen to be of the same race because they trace their ancestry back to Silesia and Poland. Among such Jews about one person in forty is a healthy carrier. Again, as in the case of sickle-cell anemia, when these carriers mate there is a 25 per cent chance of producing a child with TSD. It is now possible to take a simple blood test that will reveal whether or not an individual is a healthy carrier of the Tay-Sachs gene.

In addition to their medical importance, constitutional differences between racial populations have implications for mass production of such things as clothing. A garment manufacturer decides how long to make the sleeves and how to proportion the seat or the trouser length of a ready-made suit on the basis of averages. If these averages are compiled for one population and the garments are sold to another, the volume of requests for alterations is likely to be high. Many Blacks will find that the sleeves of garments modeled on White populations are too short. Oriental populations with their longer bodies and relatively shorter limbs will find these same sleeves too long. The experience of tailors performing alterations and minority populations buying ready-made clothes will confirm the fact of average racial differences in body build.

So it is true that medical histories and visits to the tailor can be race-related. What about behavior? Do some races have higher frequencies of genes for certain behavioral patterns than others, just as some populations have higher frequencies of genes for sickle-cell anemia or Tay-Sachs disease? The answer depends on the type of behavior. If it is a type of behavior which depends on traits whose gene frequencies vary from one racial population to another, then the answer is yes, definitely. Average population height is a good example of a race-related genetically determined trait that is important in the type of behavior known as basketball playing, an activity that places an extraordinary premium on height. Consequently taller populations such as certain Caucasoid and Black groups have a distinct genetic advantage for the practice of this behavioral pattern over shorter groups such as Mongoloids or Bushmen. And while a particular Japanese may be a superior basketball player, we expect taller populations to produce more Jerry Wests and Wilt Chamberlains.

On the other hand the decathlon is a tournament that samples an exceedingly broad spectrum of abilities including speed, endurance, body poise, and even the personality trait of determination. In an event which tests such a wide range of different abilities the particular inborn strengths of a population for one event tend to be balanced off by its inborn weaknesses for another. Hence, a decathlon winner is a rare combination of balanced excellence that is as likely to be produced by one race as another. We are not surprised to find that the list of decathlon stars includes Bob Mathias (a Caucasoid), C. K. Yang (an Oriental), and Rafer Johnson (a Black).

There are, of course, many types of behavior which do not lend themselves to such simple analysis of race-relatedness. There are behavioral characteristics which, though substantially inherited, depend upon a suitable environment for their fullest development. When one attempts to make interracial comparisons of such environment-sensitive traits between racial groups whose experience and environment differ, great difficulty is encountered in deciding to what degree the observed difference is caused by nature and therefore genetically determined and how much is a result of nurture and hence a reflection of culture and experience.

Performance on an IQ test is a type of behavior that many believe to be shaped by both heredity and environment. Interracial differences in performance on IQ tests are matters of documented fact. Here in the United States, for instance, Black populations score lower on IQ tests than White populations. Does this mean that Blacks are of inherently lower intellectual potential than Whites or does it reflect a difference in the experience or motivation of these groups? Guesses, some of them informed, have been made but no one really knows what the answer would be if Whites and Blacks shared essentially common backgrounds. The fact is that at present these groups by and large live apart, attend different schools, are motivated by different factors, and honor different values. Until all of these factors can be properly evaluated, an explanation for the observed differences in IQ scores must be delayed.

These considerations of the relationship between race and behavior point out that studies of human variation cannot produce conclusive answers when critical bits of information are unknown or unavailable and thus serve to remind us of an important point. In considering the subject of race and races understanding depends not only on knowing what is known but also on realizing what is not or cannot be known.

2

race

n general, all living things are alike. In particular, every living thing is different from every other. The unity of biology comes from the fact that the same basic principles of organization and function are shared by all life. The diversity arises from the observation that in at least some, and often in many, details of structure and function each living organism differs from every other. The variety of living things is so great that biologists have been forced to impose a system of classification on the confusing diversity of life. We all recognize that there are two great classes of living things: plants and animals. Within these two great groups, there are numerous divisions. Some animals have backbones; others do not. Some plants flower, whereas others, like mosses and molds, do not. Indeed the biologist recognizes more than a million basic subdivisions of the animal kingdom and about a third of a million such divisions of the plant kingdom. These basic subdivisions are called species.

Every species represents a particular set of solutions to the central problems of obtaining food and of reproducing that are common to all life. Each species, however, is an alternative, and in some ways unique, solution to life's challenges. Given the possibilities and constraints of a particular environment, species that represent viable adaptations will appear. Indeed, it is because we have so many different environments that we have so many species.

Members of the same species can mate and produce fertile offspring, which can in turn mate with other members of the species to produce additional fertile offspring. Under field conditions, members of different species generally cannot or will not mate. Members of the same species have many similar, even if not identical, structural and functional characteristics. That is; they look alike and act alike. Everyone recognizes the similarities of appearance and behavior that characterize members of *Canis familiaris,* the species name of man's best friend. But at the same time, everyone also recognizes the existence of clear subdivisions within this species. There are Dobermans, German shepherds, beagles, and dachshunds, just to name a few (see Figure 2-1). Even though they differ in several particulars, all these varieties of dog can interbreed to produce healthy, fertile offspring The offspring will, of course, also be members of the species *Canis familiaris* and will incorporate some of the characteristics of each parental variety.

An examination of the genetic constitution (hereditary make-up) of any of the varieties shown in Figure 2-1 reveals that the same kinds of hereditary information are present in each variety. All pass on to their descendants the information for the bone structure

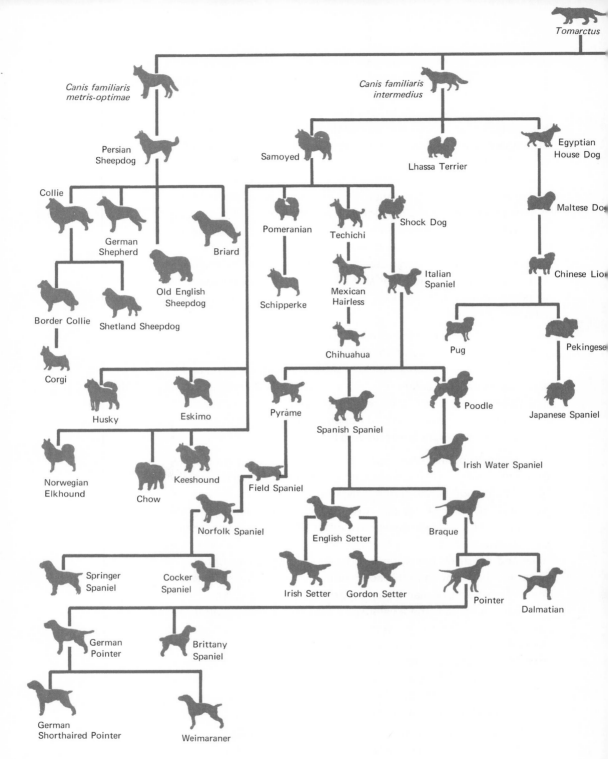

Figure 2-1
Variety and descent in the dog.

18 ∎

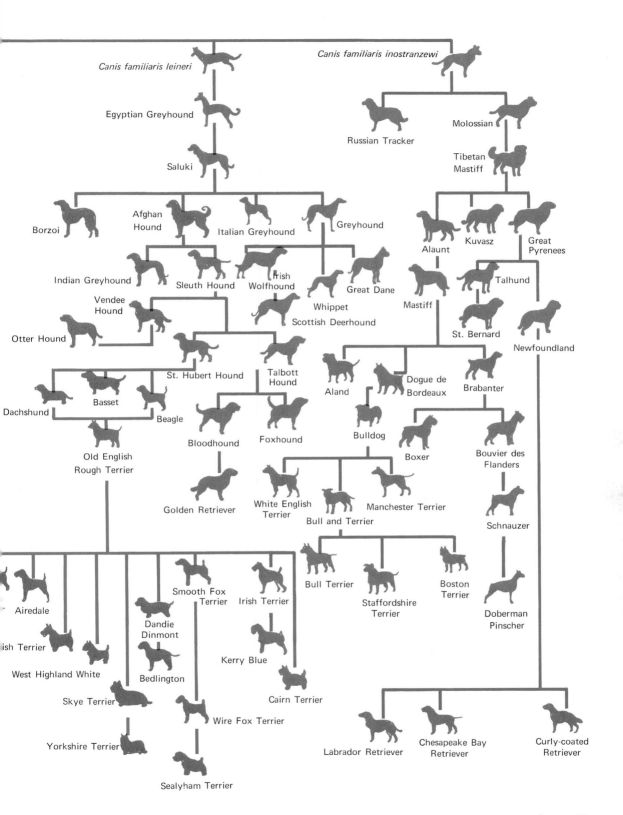

Canis familiaris leineri

Canis familiaris inostranzewi

Egyptian Greyhound

Russian Tracker

Molossian

Saluki

Tibetan Mastiff

Borzoi

Afghan Hound

Italian Greyhound

Greyhound

Alaunt

Kuvasz

Great Pyrenees

Indian Greyhound

Sleuth Hound

Irish Wolfhound

Great Dane

Mastiff

Talhund

Vendee Hound

Whippet

St. Bernard

Otter Hound

Scottish Deerhound

St. Hubert Hound

Talbott Hound

Aland

Dogue de Bordeaux

Brabanter

Newfoundland

Dachshund

Basset

Beagle

Bloodhound

Foxhound

Bulldog

Boxer

Bouvier des Flanders

Old English Rough Terrier

Golden Retriever

White English Terrier

Manchester Terrier

Schnauzer

Bull and Terrier

Airedale

Smooth Fox Terrier

Irish Terrier

Bull Terrier

Staffordshire Terrier

Boston Terrier

Doberman Pinscher

ish Terrier

Dandie Dinmont

West Highland White

Kerry Blue

Bedlington

Skye Terrier

Cairn Terrier

Wire Fox Terrier

Yorkshire Terrier

Labrador Retriever

Chesapeake Bay Retriever

Curly-coated Retriever

Sealyham Terrier

common to dogs, for a coat of hair and a pair of ears. What is striking are the different frequencies with which alternative forms of the hereditary information occur in each of the different varieties of dog. In a group of beagles, and in the descendants of beagles, the trait for a short, straight-haired coat of mosaic pattern occurs with high frequency. On the other hand, in a population of collies and in their descendants, one finds that the trait for long silky hair occurs with a very high frequency. The dachshunds are essentially defined by the peculiarities of their bone structure. A population of dachshunds is characterized by the high frequency of short stubby legs and long, low-slung bodies. Many more frequency differences for heritable traits could be catalogued. The point here is that even though the same *kinds* of traits are inherited by all dogs, different varieties of dogs are characterized by the different frequencies with which alternative forms of inherited traits appear.

How did these different frequencies of inherited traits in different breeds of dogs come to be and how are they maintained? The dachshund and the beagle were both derived by animal breeders from a common ancestor, the St. Hubert hound. In one case the breeders selected the shorter, longer-bodied offspring that appeared from time to time in the litters of the parent population of St. Hubert hounds. These short, long-bodied variants were then mated with each other. Gradually, over a number of generations, a new breeding population of short-legged, long-bodied dogs was established. It developed into the variety of dog we call the dachshund. In a similar fashion, by selecting for other characteristics, including a mosaic coat from among the offspring of St. Hubert hounds, breeders also established the population of dogs we call beagles.

We should mention here that unconsciously the breeders were establishing populations that differed from the parent population in other respects too. Different frequencies of alternative forms of other inherited traits, such as dentition (the arrangement and form of the teeth) and blood chemistry, were also established in the new varieties. And because these varieties are each maintained as breeding populations, these other differences, although unintentionally selected, have come to be as characteristic of the variety as the consciously selected patterns of coat color or bone structure. The inherited patterns that differentiate the beagle from the dachshund, and from all other varieties of dog too, will be maintained so long as beagles and dachshunds each are maintained as uniform breeding populations. If a pure population of dachshunds were regularly opened to mating with other varieties of dogs, we would obtain a more hybrid, or so-called mongrel, population. Although such mongrelization would probably improve the appearance and physique of the dachshund, it would definitely blur the distinguishing characteristics that we associate with its pure population.

Our discussion of variety in the dog helps us to formulate a definition for those different branches of the same species we call races. The races of dogs discussed here, along with races of cows (the Jersey, the Holstein, the Guernsey, and so on), chickens (White Leghorns and Rhode Island Reds), and other domestic animals, exist because of the animal breeder. Domestic animals in their present form are tailor-made products fashioned by the art and science of animal husbandry to fill man's practical needs or sometimes merely to satisfy his esthetic whims. These arranged races are to a large degree "pure" (that is to say, they are very uniform), because man tends to prune variants from the populations and to restrict mating opportunities to members of the breed. Races of sparrows, mice, or iguanas that arise in nature, usually through the geographical isolation of various populations of the same species from each other, have also been recognized and studied. They too are distinguished from each other by the different frequencies of inherited traits that exist in one breeding population in comparison with another of the same species. More often, some interbreeding occurs between members of different racial populations in nature. Consequently, one often finds that natural races, unlike the rigidly isolated races of domestic breeds, tend to be separated by intergrading zones rather than by sharp lines of demarcation. The greater degree of outbreeding notwithstanding, natural races represent distinct population groups within a species in which the preponderance of matings are, have been, and probably will be, within that population group.

Now we can formulate a definition of a race: A race is a breeding population characterized by frequencies of a collection of inherited traits that differ from those of other populations of the same species. Races are breeding populations not only in a current or instantaneous sense but also in a historical sense. Members of races represent samples from pools of inheritance, generations in depth. Whether these pools were originally filled by the conscious actions of the animal breeder or by the impersonal operation of natural forces and circumstances are considerations of mechanism, not of essence. Whether we are looking at color variation and size in wild populations of house sparrows or breeds of dogs, we are studying race.

Racial diversity is not only found among populations of dogs and sparrows; it is also common in the family of man. Members of the human family come in a variety of shapes, sizes, and colors. Some are tall, some short; some thin, some fat; some white, others black, most an intermediate hue. Clearly, although the brotherhood of man is undeniable, the brothers are not identical twins.

Surface features such as skin color, eye cast, and hair form are familiar and traditional (although not by themselves definitive) racial indicators. Our exploration of human racial biology will show that internal qualities are equally important indices of race. Indeed, internal indicators can be even more reliable than some of the traditional ones like skin color or eye cast. Appearances can be deceiving. Cosmetics can be used to change skin color. White women are fond of darkening their pale complexions with dyes that simulate suntans. Black women use bleaching creams to make their dark skins lighter. After the American occupation of Japan, a number of Japanese women underwent surgery to make their lovely almond-shaped eyes round and hard as quarters. For years Negroes applied all sorts of harsh chemicals to their hair in an operation called "konking," a chemical assault intended to straighten the hair.

We shall see, however, that no cosmetic creams or surgeon's knives are going to affect such internal indicators of race as blood type. We shall find a defining relationship between certain internal indicators and a population's racial classification. It will become apparent that the blood-group expert and the biochemist have equal authority with the morphologist in making racial assignments. The fact that blood type, bone structure, and certain details of in-ternal chemistry (in some cases, even the composition of the urine can be helpful in racial classification) differentiate human racial populations testifies to the reality and pervasiveness of race in the human species.

In our discussion of human races let us remember that race is best defined in terms of populations and the frequency with which certain inherited traits occur in particular populations as contrasted with other populations of the same species. A race is not an in-dividual marked by certain internal and external characteristics. *A race is a breeding population of individuals identifiable by the frequency with which a number of inherited traits appear in that population.* It is not the uniformity with which an inherited charac-teristic appears but rather its comparative frequency that serves to define race. This means that not every member of a race will have all the characteristics that collectively identify his racial pop-ulation. Consider this extreme example: Occasionally (about once in every 20,000 births) in populations of African Blacks a child completely lacking in pigment, and therefore white, is born. Such a child is called an albino. Even though he does not have the dark skin characteristic of the Black race, he is, racially, a Black. Further examination of this albino would certainly show that many of the other inherited indicators of race such as blood type, fingerprint pattern, and body structure are well within the guidelines for assignment to a race of Blacks.

Genetics and Race

Because races are recognized by the frequencies with which inherited traits occur in breeding populations, it is best discussed in terms of genetics. Genetics is the science that explains why like begets like and why cats always have kittens. The blueprint of instructions for the basic structure of all organisms is contained in hereditary units called genes. Just as the blueprints for the fabrication of a garage differ from those for the raising of a cathedral, the genes of a mouse are different from those of a man. The laws of genetics are based on the organization of these units, the genes, into complexes called chromosomes. Genes and groups of genes specify such characteristics as eye color, body color, height, and whether an animal will have four legs and a tail or two legs and a pair of hands. Different kinds of organisms have different kinds and different numbers of genes. A very simple organism like a virus may contain only five or ten genes; a moderately complex one like a bacterium will contain on the order of a thousand genes; and highly complex creatures like you and me may contain as many as 100,000 genes. These relationships between the gene content and the biological complexity are as expected; the more complex the structure, the more complex the blueprint.

The gene is composed of a chemical substance called deoxyribonucleic acid, or DNA. It is the most complex chemical known. Each type of gene is a DNA of slightly different chemical structure from that of every other type of gene. Thus, the nature of the gene depends on the chemical structure of its DNA. Under natural circumstances DNA is a stable and conservative structure that does not readily undergo change. When the DNA of a gene suffers a change in structure, the information content of the gene is altered and the alteration may be transmitted to future generations. Such permanent, heritable alterations in the genetic material are called mutations. Under natural circumstances they are rare; the chances that a mutation will occur in a particular gene are usually less than one in 100,000. But although they are rare, mutations have occurred

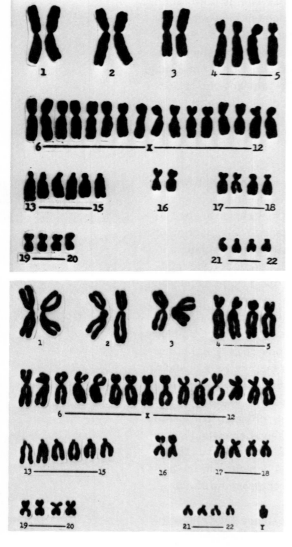

Figure 2-2
The human chromosome complement (called the karyotype). Top, the karyotype of a normal human female; bottom, the karyotype of a normal human male.

in the past, they are occurring now, and they constitute an important source of the variation so characteristic of living organisms.

Genes are arranged in a linear order, like boxcars in a freight train, into units called chromosomes. Every organism has at least one chromosome. Many organisms, like ourselves, have several. As shown in Figure 2-2, man has 23 pairs of chromosomes, or a total of 46. One of these 23 pairs is involved in sex determination. The sex chromosomes are of two types, X and Y. A female has two X chromosomes, a male one X and one Y. The other 22 pairs of chromosomes, which are not involved in sex determination, are called autosomes.

A child inherits one set of 23 chromosomes from his mother and a complementary set of 23 from his father (see Detail Diagram 1). This is why offspring resemble their parents. Part of the same genetic blueprints that specified the basic design of each parent also specifies the structure of the offspring. Therefore, cats must have kittens and sons and daughters must resemble their mothers and fathers. But even though we expect a resemblance between parents and their offspring, we have also come to expect a degree of variation. We know that children are not identical to their parents but differ from them in a number of respects. The genetic heritage of each child is determined at the moment of fertilization when a sperm from the father carrying half the child's genes unites with an egg in the mother that contains the other half. Therefore, although every child is genetically similar to either parent, he is identical to neither. Each child is a hybrid. Note also that each parent is also a hybrid of genes from the child's grandparents. Thus, each generation is in fact a genetic mixture of genetic mixtures, a hybrid of hybrids. It is in this unceasing shuffle of chromosomes and genes that we find the significance of sex. It is nature's way of looking for a winning combination. And because today's winner may be a loser in tomorrow's environment (consider the dinosaur), variation — the raw material of evolution — is guaranteed by the gene shuffle of sexual reproduction.

With this background of genetics we can enlarge our understanding of race by noting that in a historically breeding population the same genes (but not the same gene combinations) are being exchanged by individuals in that population. Because gene is a formal and, more importantly, precise way of saying inherited trait, we can restate the definition of race as follows:

A race is a breeding population characterized by gene frequencies different from those of other populations of the same species. The term breeding population *is usually intended in a historic as well as a current sense.*

Detail Diagram 1
Fertilization and genetics (see pages 26, 27).

Each child is the end product of a succession of fertilizations, the hybrid offspring of parents that were themselves hybrids.

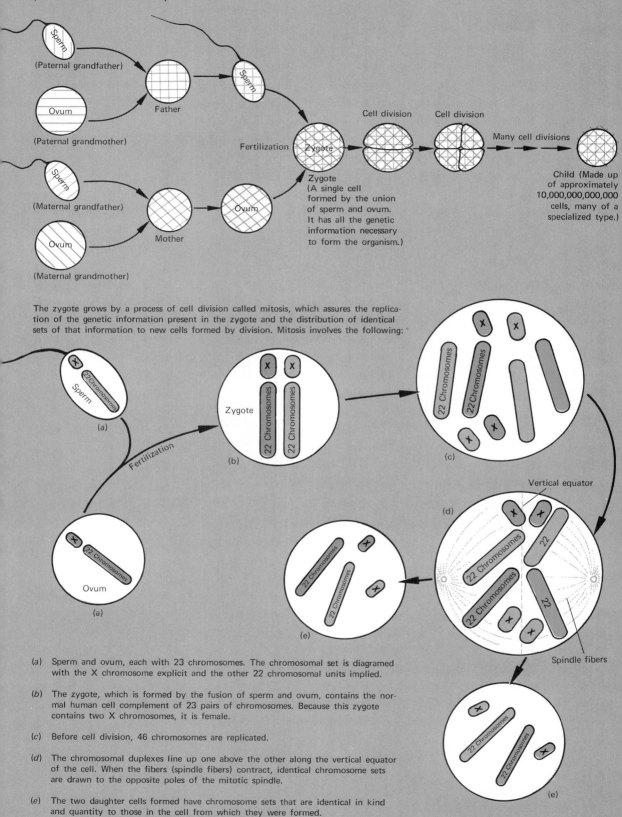

The zygote grows by a process of cell division called mitosis, which assures the replication of the genetic information present in the zygote and the distribution of identical sets of that information to new cells formed by division. Mitosis involves the following:

(a) Sperm and ovum, each with 23 chromosomes. The chromosomal set is diagramed with the X chromosome explicit and the other 22 chromosomal units implied.

(b) The zygote, which is formed by the fusion of sperm and ovum, contains the normal human cell complement of 23 pairs of chromosomes. Because this zygote contains two X chromosomes, it is female.

(c) Before cell division, 46 chromosomes are replicated.

(d) The chromosomal duplexes line up one above the other along the vertical equator of the cell. When the fibers (spindle fibers) contract, identical chromosome sets are drawn to the opposite poles of the mitotic spindle.

(e) The two daughter cells formed have chromosome sets that are identical in kind and quantity to those in the cell from which they were formed.

Formation of the gametes. Gametes are sperm in the testes of men and ova in the ovaries of women. The gametes are formed by a process of cell division called meiosis, which produces genetically distinct cells with only half the 46 chromosomes found in other human cells.

(a)
The first step in meiosis involves chromosome duplication. Each chromosome directs the production of an exact replica of itself. This cell has a total of 46 chromosomal units.

(b)
This cell has 92 chromosomal units.

(c)
In meiosis each of the newly replicated chromosome bundles pairs with its homologous newly replicated chromosome bundle. Thus the X's pair with the X's, and similarly, each of the other 22 chromosome bundles pair. During the pairing the chromosomes exchange pieces in a process called crossing over.

(e)
The spindle fibers then contract and pull the opposing chromosome duplexes apart. The cell begins to divide into two cells, each of which has 46 chromosomal units. Notice that because of the transformations, such as crossing over, that accompany meiosis, the chromosome set is different from that in the parent germ cell.

(d)
The chromosomes move to the vertical equator of the cell. Each of the duplexes becomes aligned across the cell equator from its homologous duplex. Each alignment is independent.

(f)
In this second division the chromosomes of the duplexes are separated from each other and segregated into the gametes.

(g)
Each of the gametes, or sex cells, contains only half (23) the number of chromosomal units that were present in the parental cell.

22 Chromosomes

X

X

Other 22 chromosomes

X

X

22 Chromosomes

22 Chromosomes

X

X

Other 22 chromosomes

Other 22 chromosomes

X

X

X

X

X

X

X

X

X

X

X

X

X

X

X

X

X

X

X

X

22

X

X

22

22

X

22

X

3
races

f we put members of the human species into groups according to physical characteristics, we can arrive at a number of branches, called races, that will overlap each other to some extent. Almost everyone's classification will include three large groups: the Mongoloid, the Caucasoid, and the Negroid. A careful survey of the peoples of the earth or a few conversations with some of those who have made a study of racial diversity would lead one to expand the list. One would add a category, the Australoid, to accommodate the aboriginal populations of Australia, the Malay Peninsula, and some of the neighboring island chains. The Capoid category should also be added to accommodate the Bushmen, that short-statured and dying race of the Kalahari. A category must be set up to include those populations native to the Western Hemisphere, the American Indian. A catalogue of the varieties of man would certainly include that exotic and ornamental people aboriginal to Hawaii and other Pacific islands, the Polynesians. Indeed a careful study of the major categories—Caucasoid, Mongoloid, and Negroid—reveals that they are in reality racial conglomerates, each containing a diversity of breeding populations. Before our list is complete we shall have listed more than two dozen racial varieties of man. If this seems a great many, we should remember that on the order of 150 different varieties of the pocket gopher, *Thomomys bottae,* have been described. There are more than a hundred distinct breeds of dogs, dozens of breeds of cattle, and literally countless varieties of fruit flies or leopard frogs. The interesting question is probably why there are so few rather than so many readily distinguished races of man.

The next few pages contain a pictorial survey of the major races of man. From a study of these illustrations it will be apparent that within any given race there is an enormous amount of variation. This variation within any group is sufficiently great that we can find a substantial amount of overlap between all the major categories. We should not be surprised to find a blurring of the lines of racial demarcation. Because there has been a great deal of gene flow between human populations, none of the major races is pure.

The Mongoloids ("Yellow Man")

Skin color in the Mongoloid group actually ranges from nearly white through an apparent yellow to brown. In this group, as in so many others, one can make an approximate correlation between

Figure 3-1
THE MONGOLOIDS

Chinese children

Tsung Dao Lee — Nobel laureate

Chinese: old and young

Tsung-Dao Lee

A young Chinese woman

Chief Thundercloud—An American Indian

A Korean school

Figure 3-1 *(Cont.)*
THE MONGOLOIDS

Tibetan man with prayer trumpet

Chen Ning Yang — Nobel laureate

Hideki Yukawa — Nobel laureate

A middle-aged American Indian woman

the latitude in which a people live and their skin color. The lighter-skinned variations are found to be more prevelant in the North, whereas the darker-skinned groups tend to be found in the South in and near the tropics. The hair of the Mongoloids tends to be black, of large diameter, and round, and it grows long on the head. Heavy beards and generously distributed body hair are uncommon among these peoples. Their faces are characterized by high, prominent cheek bones and almond-shaped eyes that are brown to black. In Mongoloid populations the faces are often relatively flat. A wide range of statures is found: some subgroups are quite tall, whereas others average only a little over five feet in height. The body build is often characterized by a long torso with relatively short arms and legs. Hands and feet tend to be small. To these general character-istics (shown in Figure 3-1) we might add some special anatomical features that are distinctive of these groups. The fingernails when viewed from the side appear curved, and the inside surface of the incisors of many members of this group are concave or "shoveled." Examination of the map in Figure 3-2 shows the area in which the various groups included in the Mongoloid race are most greatly concentrated. On the basis of close study of this group, some anthropologists and population geneticists have proposed that it be subdivided into five groups:

1. North Chinese—northern and central China and Manchuria.
2. Classic Mongoloid—Siberia, Mongolia, Korea, and Japan.
3. Southeast Asian—South China, Thailand, Viet Nam, Burma, and Indonesia.
4. Tibetan—Tibet.
5. American Indian—the indigenous populations of North, South, and Central America.

The Caucasoids ("White Man")

Although most people would equate the terms *Caucasoid* and *White,* those who have made a study of race and races are inclined not to form such an equation. In the Caucasoid group, as in the Mongoloid, one finds a wide range of skin color; it varies from the pale, translucent, alabaster white of the Scandinavian through the Mediterranean tan of the Greek to the brown of the Arab. Similarly, eye color among the Caucasoids ranges from the blue so common in Sweden to the dark brown characteristic of the Greek and Arab. The hair of the Caucasoids, which can be found in a spectrum of colors—yellow, red, brown, black—is usually straight or wavy.

Although there is great variation in the structure of the nose, ranging from high and narrow to broad and snub, the lips are usually thin. Many of the males can grow heavy beards and there are large

Figure 3-2

The geographic occurrence of the 26 races of man. (1) Northwest European; (2) Northeast European; (3) Alpine; (4) Mediterranean; (5) Pakistani and Indian; (6) Tibetan; (7) North Chinese; (8) Classic Mongoloid; (9) Eskimo; (10) Southeast Asian; (11) North American Indian; (12) South American Indian; (13) East African; (14) West African; (15) Bantu; (16) Bushman and Hottentot; (17) African Pygmy; (18) Southern India and Ceylon; (19) Negrito; (20) Melanesian-Papuan; (21) Australoid; (22) Micronesian; (23) Polynesian; (24) Neo-Hawaiian; (25) Black American; (26) South African Colored. (After T. Dobzhansky, in Mankind Evolving. *New Haven, Conn.: Yale University Press, 1962.)*

amounts of body hair. There is a tendency to early baldness in many males, and the hair tends to gray in the thirties and forties. In Caucasoids one finds a variable body build, from the medium-short stature of Mediterranean populations to the tallness of some Scandinavian groups. In general the torso tends to be relatively long and ranges from relatively heavy and fleshy to small and wiry. This group, which includes a wide diversity of types (see Figure 3-3), can be divided into the following four subcategories, which more nearly approximate breeding populations:

1. Northwest European — Scandinavia, northern Germany, Netherlands, Great Britain, and Ireland.
2. Northeast European — Russia, Poland.
3. Alpine — France, southern Germany, Switzerland, northern Italy, Yugoslavia, Balkans.

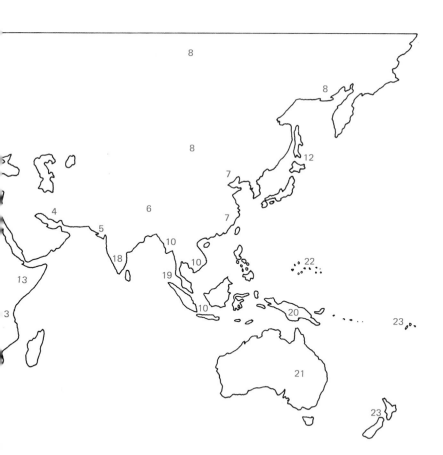

Figure 3-3
THE CAUCASOIDS

A group of Germans

Albert Schweitzer — Nobel laureate

A young American woman

Albert Schweitzer

A group of German children

An elderly woman of Finland

An American boy

Linus Pauling — Nobel laureate

A group of Turks

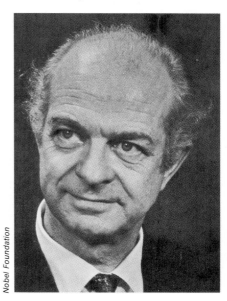

Figure 3-3 *(Cont.)*
THE CAUCASOIDS

A group of Persians

Iranian Embassy

Melvin Calvin — Nobel laureate

A New Zealand man of advanced years

4. Mediterranean—peoples from both sides of the Mediterranean, from Tangiers to the Dardanelles, including Arabia, Turkey, and Iran.

The Negroids ("Black Man")

The Negroid group is characterized by color and body build (see Figure 3-4). Skin color ranges from brown to black, as does that of the hair and eyes. The hair on the head is often tightly curled; the body hair is sparsely distributed. Full lips, broad noses, small close-set ears, and relatively rounded heads are common in this group. The body build is characteristically long limbed, with larger hands and feet than those of Mongoloid and many Caucasoid groups. Within this group one finds a greater spread in height than in the first two groups, ranging from the towering Watussi, some of whom are as tall as seven feet, to the pygmies, small folk of the forest whose adult height is under five feet. This broad racial category, like the Mongoloid and Caucasoid, is best divided into smaller groups that more nearly approximate breeding populations. We can recognize the following groups:

1. The North American Black—the so-called Negro population of North America. Even though the majority of its genes (80 per cent) come from African Black populations, it contains a significant percentage (20 per cent) of Caucasoid genes from Europe. There is no evidence of an appreciable contribution from the Indian populations indigenous to America. This is a relatively new breeding population resulting from an African Black-European hybridization.
2. South American Black—a significant fraction of the Brazilian population. These people, like the North American Black, have a genetic background that is predominantly African Black but with an admixture of European and South American Indian as well.
3. Sub-Saharan African
    a. West African Black—West Africa and much of the Congo.
    b. Bantu—Mozambique, Angola, parts of the Union of South Africa, and lower East Africa.
    c. East African Black—Kenya, Tanzania, parts of the Sudan and Ethiopia.
    d. Forest Pygmy—the rain forests of equatorial Africa.
    e. Hottentot—the name given the aboriginal inhabitants of South Africa by colonizing Dutchmen.

Figure 3-4
THE BLACKS

A pair of West Africans

Ralph Bunche—Nobel laureate

An American Black school child

Martin Luther King, Jr. – Nobel laureate

An American Black farm boy

New York Public Library, Schomburg Collection

A young Black woman
of the Lesser Antilles

Figure 3-4 *(Cont.)*
THE BLACKS

*Albert John Lutuli
—Nobel laureate*

An American Black man

A middle-aged American Black woman

Peoples of the Indian Subcontinent

Although not so widely dispersed as the Caucasoids, the Mongoloids, or the Negroids, the group of populations of the Indian subcontinent comprises one of the major varieties of man. Indeed, these peoples, numbering some 500 million, are more numerous than the various Negroid peoples. After the Mongoloid and Caucasoid, this group of populations is collectively the third most numerous variety of man. Their skin color ranges from light through medium brown to black. Hair is straight or wavy, and black. Eyes are brown to black, lips thin to medium full, and cheek bones are distinct. Although some, especially among the northern Indian populations, are tall, body builds are usually of medium height and slender (see Figure 3-5). These two subpopulations (which could be further subdivided) can be recognized:

1. The people of Pakistan and much of India.
2. The people of southern India and the island of Ceylon.

Other Groups

In addition to the four major racial groups and their subgroups there are a number of other groups of men that are not nearly so numerous but are certainly as distinct.

The Capoids.   The Capoid group, which contains the Bushmen of South Africa, seems to be a disappearing race of man; fewer than 100,000 individuals can be counted in Bushman populations today. Their stature ranges from five feet to just a little less than five and a half feet. They have brown to yellowish skin and flat faces. Their hair is often tightly coiled into spiral tufts; in the males it is mostly confined to the head and beard and is very sparsely distributed over the rest of the body. For their height, they have relatively long bodies with short limbs. The hands and feet are characteristically small. Some members of this group are distinguished by large fat pads (steatopygia) on the buttocks (Figure 3-6).

The Australoids.   The Australoid group is found in parts of Australia, New Guinea, and some other sections of the far-western Pacific. Its members range in color from nearly black to medium and light brown. The hair, which can vary from tightly coiled to straight, is widely distributed over the body, as is true of the Caucasoid group. Although the hair is usually black, in some parts of the Australian desert one can find blond hair, especially in women and children. This race is characterized by deep-set eyes, a large

Figure 3-5
*PEOPLES OF
THE INDIAN
SUBCONTINENT*

Indian Embassy

Nobel Foundation

Prime Minister Indira Gandhi, an Indian lady

Chandrasekhara Venkata Raman — Nobel laureate

Indian children

Indian Embassy

Young Ceylonese women

United Nations

A group of Ceylonese

Ceylonese Embassy

Rabindranath Tagore — Nobel laureate

Nobel Foundation

Figure 3-5 *(Cont.)*
*PEOPLES OF THE
INDIAN SUBCONTINENT*

*Cyril Ponnamperuma
— Ceylonese chemist
and authority on
chemical evolution*

Nobel Foundation

*H. Gobind Khorana
— Nobel laureate*

*Mohandas K. Gandhi
— philosopher, liberator,
and martyr*

Indian Embassy

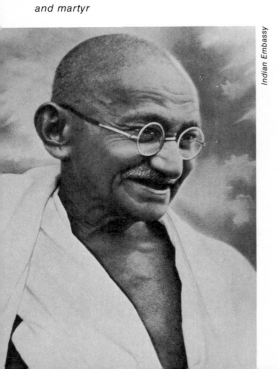

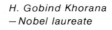

prominent nose, and full lips. As in the case of the Caucasoids, hair in this group tends to gray and the males tend to bald relatively early in adult life. They vary in height from the medium range of 5 feet, 6 inches to 5 feet, 8 inches down to the pygmy size of five feet (Figure 3-6).

Melanesians, Negritos, Micronesians, and Polynesians. From Hawaii through the Western Pacific into Micronesia and into parts of the Philippines we find a variety of people who are believed by some anthropologists to represent combinations in various proportions of persons of Australoid and Mongoloid stock. These people include the Polynesians of Hawaii and the Fiji Islands, the Melanesians of New Guinea, and the Micronesians of Saipan and Guam. Their skin colors vary from light brown to black, and they range in size from the Negritos of New Guinea and the Philippines, slightly under five feet, to the tall Hawaiian Islanders (see Figure 3-6). We can list the following groups:

1. Melanesian — Pacific islands, from New Guinea to Fiji.
2. Micronesian — islands of the western Pacific.
3. Polynesian — islands of the central and eastern Pacific, notably Hawaii.
4. Negrito — a small-statured, frizzly-haired, and dark-skinned people distributed from the Philippines to New Guinea.

The noted student of race Carleton Coon has said, "Not every person in the world can be tapped on the shoulder and told, 'You belong to such and such a race'." After an examination of the preceding album of race, the reader will probably agree with this statement. Among groups of Caucasoids one sees a face here and there with strongly Mongoloid overtones and occasionally one with the full lips or kinky hair of the Negro. In groups of black Africans, one sometimes finds atop a classically Negroid body, a classically Caucasoid head. These frequent exceptions to the general characteristics that delineate racial groups are not disturbing and require little reflection to explain. Man is a single species, and so, when the opportunity presents itself, members of different races often interbreed and sometimes even intermarry. The frequent failure to exchange marital vows has not prevented populations from exchanging genes. Once introduced into a population the new genes, although diluted, may nevertheless surface from time to time. It is for this reason that descriptions of the races of man are at best general idealizations to which one must match groups of real men. We must understand that the assignment of men to racial categories, even though it is a real and possible exercise in judgment, is in many cases only an approximate one.

Figure 3-6
*OTHER RACIAL
GROUPS*

An Australoid man

A group of young Negritos of Bataan

A Melanesian man of the Solomon Islands

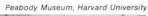

Two Bushman women and their children

A Polynesian man of New Zealand

4

the
depth
of
diversity

t is true that one can group men approximately according to race by means of careful visual examination. Enough differences exist in color, hair form, facial features, and body type to allow a careful student of race to make racial assignments, even though he cannot be completely accurate, on the basis of detailed visual examination. A moment's reflection will suggest that these visually observable differences in color, build, and facial cast must have a deeper constitutional basis. Such obvious differences in observable structure must be more than skin deep and would be expected to be manifested in the internal structure and chemistry of the individual. One could imagine an experiment to determine whether or not racial distinctions are only those of outward appearance or whether there exist internal as well as external constitutional differences that would allow one to recognize members of races as certainly as do differences in outward appearance.

Suppose, for example, three hundred people—one hundred of them Chinese, one hundred Black Africans, and one hundred Caucasians from northern Europe—split up into their various groups and each race entered a room of its own. Could we, sight unseen, determine which room held the Chinese, the Blacks, and the Whites? The answer is that we could, definitely, provided that each individual in these various groups were willing to help us by supplying the following: (1) a sample of ear wax; (2) a urine sample; (3) a few drops of blood; (4) a set of fingerprints; and (5) information about whether or not he could taste a particular compound, PTC.[1] All these indicators, with the exception of the fingerprint, reflect the internal chemistry and constitution of the individual. If we then survey what is already known about the racial patterns that have been observed for these indicators, we would accomplish two purposes: First, we would discover that, given the services of a blood-group expert, a biochemist, and someone skilled in the interpretation of fingerprints, the bit of detective work we set for ourselves is easily accomplished. Secondly, we would have a convincing demonstration that race, unlike beauty, is more than skin deep.

Ear Wax

Some years ago it was discovered that there are two types of ear wax: one form is crumbly and dry, and the other is moist and

Some Racial Indicators

[1] PTC—phenylthiocarbamide, a chemical compound that has a slightly bitter taste.

Table 4-1.

Percentage of Population Bearing the Dry Ear Wax Gene

Adapted from E. Matsunaga, *Annals of Human Genetics,* **25**(1962) pp. 277–286.

Population Examined	Percentage Bearing Gene
Northern Chinese	98
Southern Chinese	86
Japanese	92
Melanesians	53
Micronesians	61
Germans	18
American Whites	16
American Negroes	7

adhesive. Furthermore, an examination of individuals from different parts of the world soon showed that it was possible to establish a relationship between the individual's racial ancestry and his type of ear wax. Just as one inherits characteristics of outward appearance, such as eye cast and hair form, one also inherits the capacity to form a particular type of ear wax. These studies demonstrated that among East Asian populations, such as Chinese and Japanese, the dry crumbly kind of ear wax is formed almost exclusively. On the other hand, in Caucasians and particularly in Negroes, the adhesive form predominates and the dry form is rarely found. Table 4-1 shows the striking differences that are found when Mongoloid populations are contrasted with Caucasoid and Negroid populations.

Tasters and Nontasters

Many people are able to taste the bitter flavor of PTC, a compound that, along with some related substances, has antithyroid activity. Bits of filter paper can be impregnated with a dilute solution of PTC and given to subjects to see if they can detect its slightly bitter taste. The majority of individuals in any racial population can taste PTC. However, the size of the majority tends to vary among racial groups (see Table 4-2). One finds the lowest percentage of tasters among the Australian aborigines and the highest percentages among Mongoloids and Negroes.

Table 4-2.

Percentage of PTC Tasters in Different Populations

Adapted from Carleton S. Coon, *The Living Races of Man* (New York: Alfred A. Knopf, 1965), p. 264.

Group	Percentage of Tasters
Europeans	60–80
Negroes	90–97
East Asians (Chinese, Japanese, and related populations)	83–100
Australian Aborigines	50–70
Micronesians	70–80

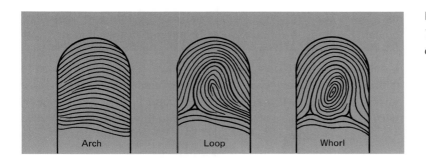

Figure 4-1
*Three basic types
of fingerprints.*

Fingerprints

Fingerprints represent patterns that are present at birth and do not change throughout the remainder of life. They consist of a pattern of loops, arches, and whorls that is characteristic of each individual. However, identical twins have identical fingerprints and related individuals have similar fingerprints. The degree of similarity between the fingerprints of two individuals can be used as an index of kinship. The closer the kin, the more similar the fingerprints. It is not surprising, therefore, to find that fingerprint patterns can be correlated with race. Many surveys recording the distribution of basic patterns of loops, whorls, and arches in various populations have been made (see Figure 4-1). The data in Table 4-3 show that a preponderance of loops characterizes Caucasoid and African populations, whereas Mongoloids have more whorls than loops.

Urine

Urine, like blood, is an indicator of internal body chemistry. Everyone is familar with the use of urinalysis to detect the body's inability to handle sugar properly because of diabetes. It is also

Group	Arches	Loops	Whorls
European	0–9	63–76	20–42
Negroes	3–12	53–73	20–40
Bushmen	13–16	66–68	15–21
East Asians (Chinese, Japanese, and related populations)	1–5	43–56	44–54
American Indians	2–8	46–61	35–57
Australian Aborigines	0–1	28–46	52–73
Micronesians	2	49	49–50

Table 4-3.
*Percentage Range
of Types of Finger-
prints Among
Populations*

Adapted from Carleton S.
Coon, *The Living Races
of Man* (New York: Alfred
A. Knopf, 1965), p. 261.

possible to use urinalysis to discover more subtle and nonpatho- logical variations in other aspects of internal body chemistry from one individual to another. For instance, a compound that readily is detected in the biochemistry laboratory, beta-amino-isobutyric acid (BAIB), is rarely excreted in large amounts by Europeans; however, excess BAIB excretion is common in Asians and among many groups of American Indians, who are thought to be derivative populations of older Asian groups.

In a comparative study of the urinary excretion patterns of two different racial populations, one Negro, the other Caucasoid, living under standardized conditions, differences were found. On the basis of the pattern of amino acid excretion, it was possible to separate the Negro population from the Caucasoid. Because the subjects in this investigation lived together and took their meals together, it is reasonable to suggest that the observed differences in the patterns of amino acid excretion are genetic in origin.

Blood

The familiar and life-saving technique of blood transfusion was impossible seventy years ago. Many of the numerous attempts to transfuse blood before 1900 resulted in the death of the recipient. Although occasionally a recipient survived a transfusion, it was highly probable that random combinations of donors and recipients would have blood incompatibilities. Then in the early 1900s Karl Landsteiner discovered what the clinician's experience had sug- gested was likely, that there are different blood types. We have come to know these four different blood groups as A, B, AB, and O.[2] All human blood types can be at least partially described as belonging to a subdivision of these four main categories. We inherit our blood type from our parents. The accompanying chart indicates how these types are inherited and what the basis is for blood incompatibilities (see Detail Diagram 2). Taken the world over, the most common blood type is O. The other groups, depending on geographic locality, are found in greater or lesser frequency. Blood group A is the next most frequent and B is the least common of the three A, B, O types.

The Rh factor, which is especially important in pregnancy, provides yet another important index for blood classification. The Rh factor was discovered when Landsteiner and his associate Wiener injected blood from a Rhesus monkey into rabbits and guinea pigs. Later an examination of the serum from these animals

[2]In the years since the discovery of the A, B, O groups, another set of determinants known as the N, M, S, U system has been discovered and studied extensively.

Table 4-4. *Blood-Group Variation (Percentages) Among Populations*

Population	A_1	A_2	B	O	Rh Negative	Duffy Factor
Caucasians	5–40	1–37	4–18	45–75	25–46	37–82
Negroes	8–30	1–8	10–20	52–70	4–29	0–6
East Asians	0–45	0–5	16–25	39–68	0–5	90–100
American Indians	0–20	about 0	0–4	68–100	about 0	22–99

Adapted from Carleton S. Coon, *The Living Races of Man* (New York: Alfred A. Knopf, 1965), p. 286.

showed that it contained antibodies that would cause agglutination of the red cells in fresh samples of Rhesus monkey blood. Further investigation revealed that 85 per cent of the blood samples from a population of Caucasoid New Yorkers reacted with the serum by agglutinating. Fifteen out of every one hundred samples showed no reaction. This observation established the existence of yet another typing marker on the surface of red blood cells — the Rh factor. The 85 per cent of the population whose blood cells reacted with this typing serum were said to be Rh positive and the 15 per cent that did not were labeled Rh negative, as indicated in Table 4-4. The transfusion of Rh positive blood into an Rh negative individual can cause complications due to incompatibility. But Rh factor complications are not limited to blood transfusions. Matings between Rh positive males and Rh negative females can produce Rh positive offspring. Repeated pregnancies in Rh negative mothers initiated by Rh positive fathers can be especially dangerous. The mother's blood has produced antibodies that give her an immunity to the blood of any Rh positive fetuses carried during early pregnancies. These antibodies in her blood can then attack and damage any Rh positive fetuses in later pregnancies.

About twenty years ago another blood group factor, known as the Duffy factor, was discovered in Australia. It is common among Koreans, Chinese, Japanese, and Australoids and is found in about half the whites and only about ten per cent of those populations whose ancestry can be traced to Sub-Saharan Africa. Such a spectrum of racial distribution makes it a useful gene for establishing blood-group related racial classifications. These considerations of race-related blood-group differences are summarized in Table 4-4.

Clearly, those blood types we should observe most carefully in Table 4-4 are A_2, Rh negative, and Duffy. We find that Caucasians have more Rh negatives than any other major racial group: they also have more A_2. Negroes have a lower frequency of Rh negatives than Caucasians, but a significantly higher one than Orientals; they are distinctive in their low frequency of the Duffy factor. If we look at the proportions of Rh negatives, type A_2, and Duffy

Detail Diagram 2
The ABO blood groups: Their incompatibility relationships and genetics (see pages 60, 61).

(A) Incompatibility Relationships in the ABO System. Whole blood can be separated into serum and red blood cells. Mixing serum or whole blood from donors of one blood type with red blood cells or whole blood from an individual of a different type may result in an incompatibility reaction. For instance, when serum or whole blood from a type A individual is mixed with red blood cells or whole blood cells from a type B individual, the red blood cells clump together or agglutinate.

Type B
red blood cells
(unagglutinated).

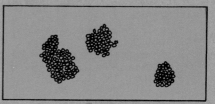

Type B red blood cells that
have been agglutinated by
addition of type A serum
or whole blood.

The agglutination reaction takes place because the type A serum contains substances known as anti-B antibodies, which react with materials called type B antigens present on the surface of type B blood cells. This reaction between antigen and antibody causes the red blood cells to stick to each other, as shown in the diagram.

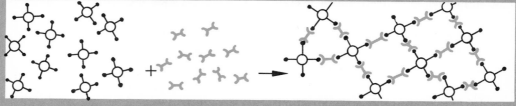

Type B red blood cells   Type A antigen   Agglutination

(B) General Summary of Incompatibility Relationships for the Blood Groups

Blood group	Antigens carried on the red blood cells	Antiblood group antigens present in the serum	Reaction with serum from a donor of this type: O A B AB	Persons with the blood type indicated in the first column:	
				Can donate blood to persons of this blood type:	Can receive blood donations from this blood type:
O	O	Anti-A Anti-B		O, A, B, and AB	Only O
A	A	Anti-B		A and AB	O and A
B	B	Anti-A		B and AB	O and B
AB	AB	———		AB only	O, A, B, and AB

(C) The Inheritance of the ABO Blood Groups

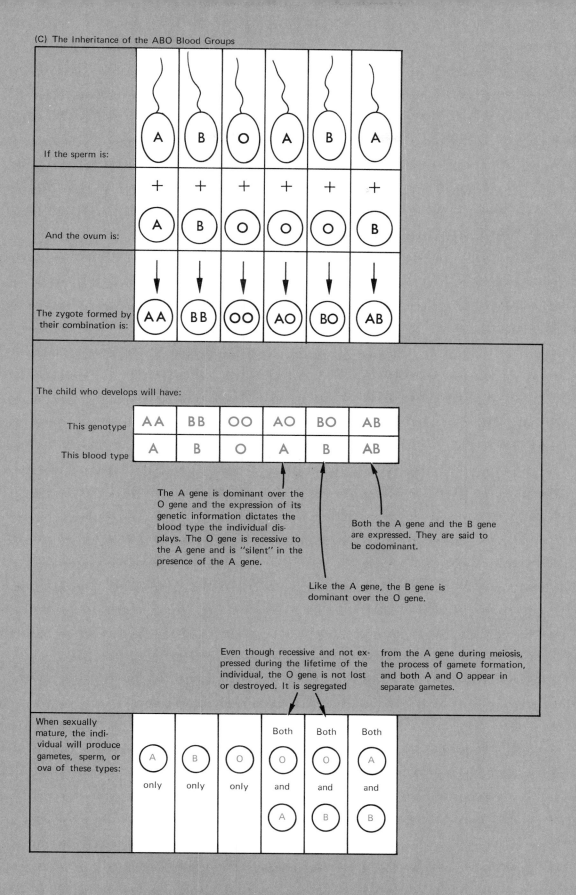

positives we can identify the East Asian group. This group, like the American Indian, has few Rh negative individuals. Among East Asians there is a high frequency of Duffy positives and fewer A_2 individuals than are found among Caucasians and Negroes. The American Indian is markedly blood type O, and rarely Rh negative or type A_2.

A Practical Example of the Definition of a Race as a Population

This discussion of blood types provides a useful opportunity to examine our definition of race in terms of gene frequencies in populations rather than in terms of the characteristics of an isolated individual. The blood-group frequencies listed here describe populations, not individuals. A blood bank would be criminally negligent if it assumed that each pint of blood collected from American Indians was type O. It is true that for the group as a whole, type O blood predominates, but an individual Indian may have type A or type B blood. Each individual pint of blood must be tested and evaluated individually without regard to the blood-type characteristics of the population. A detailed knowledge of the population genetics of the American Indians would not allow one to determine, with certainty, the blood type of a particular American Indian. To assume that one could prejudge the blood type without benefit of direct measurement would endanger the recipient of the transfusion. The need to distinguish between group and individual characteristics applies to more than blood. What is true of blood groups is true of other genetically and culturally inherited traits. To know the particulars of the population is not to know the particulars of an individual in the population.

Perspective

So far much has been made of the average differences that can easily be found when comparing one racial group with another. Some perspective on the magnitude of the differences between groups can be gained by exploring the average differences seen within racial groups. Suppose we have two Caucasoid individuals, W and w, picked at random, and two Blacks, B and b, selected in a similarly random fashion. What is the magnitude of the genetic difference between W and w or B and b, as compared to the average difference between Caucasoids and Blacks as a group? It turns out that the comparison can be made by examining the differences in chemical structure of the proteins produced by two different individuals or by two different racial populations. This is because almost every gene of an organism specifies the detailed structure of one of the many thousands of different types of proteins that play their various roles, as diverse as digestion and defense, in maintaining the integrity of the body. Consequently, differences in proteins taken from two different sources can be used as a measure of the genetic differences between those sources. The distinguished geneticist L. L. Cavalli-Sforza has pointed out that such analyses have shown that an average difference of about 0.02 per cent will be found between members of the same racial population.[3] Compare this with the magnitude of the difference, about 1 per cent, when we humans are compared with our nearest primate relatives, the chimpanzees. Pursuing this type of investigation, we find that the average difference between two racial groups, such as Blacks and Whites, or Whites and Chinese, will be on the order of slightly more than 0.02 per cent — in absolute terms, just a little more than the variation between members of the same race. Two lessons can be learned from these observations. First, there is considerable variation between human beings, whether they belong to the same racial group or not. Secondly, racial differences add very little to the variation that already exists between human beings.

Seeing these differences in perspective does not gainsay our original observation that racial differences are pervasive and penetrating. The list of constitutional and internal racial differences we have examined in this chapter could be extended even further if we considered such characteristics as bone structure. The documentation of external and internal differences in human populations leads one to wonder about the origin and meaning of these variations. Why are there races of men and where did they come from? A final, detailed, and demonstrably valid answer to these questions cannot be given now. Nor will it be given ten or even fifty years from now. It is not possible to have a delayed replay of the origin of today's races of man. What is possible is to build a rational framework for considering the origin of races. The foundation for such a framework is evolution and man's emergence as a consequence of its operation. It is man's evolution and his differentiation into racial varieties that we will consider in the next two chapters.

[3]0.02 per cent may seem like a small number until one realizes that in absolute terms it represents around 200,000 differences in the approximately five billion DNA base pairs that encode the genetic information necessary to specify a human being.

5

evolution
and
man

A little more than one hundred years ago, in 1859, Charles Darwin published a book called *The Origin of Species.* In it he advanced a carefully supported theory of evolution. The inevitable conclusion of the theory of evolution is that all the different kinds of living things we see in the world today descended by gradual modification from ancestors quite unlike themselves, generations removed. The community of life as we see it today arose from other life forms, many of which have become extinct. Living things as different as men and fish can trace a different kinship back through tens of thousands of generations to a common ancestor. If you followed your family tree back through enough generations, you would find some ancestors that were not human.

During the hundred years since the publication of *The Origin of Species,* this theory has survived attacks from political, religious, and scientific quarters. Denunciations from political and religious opponents have largely subsided. It would appear that most of these critics have suffered either evolution or extinction. Criticism from scientists has spurred the proponents of the theory to the discovery of new evidence, thus the evolutionary point of view has been strengthened and extended, not weakened. Indeed, so persuasive is the evidence for evolution that now it is not viewed as hypothesis or conjecture but stands as one of the established laws of biology.

Evolution operates through the mechanism of natural selection. Natural selection has been described as being comprised of three critical elements: First of all, in nature individuals differ among themselves. Secondly, genetic factors that can be passed on from one generation to the next are to some extent responsible for these naturally occurring differences. And thirdly, whenever these genetically determined differences affect fitness, the individuals who are genetically more fit will be increasingly represented in succeeding generations. An appreciation of evolutionary processes depends on an understanding of natural selection. To understand natural selection one must have a clear understanding of fitness.

Fitness

If we recall the process of fertilization, we will remember that a portion of each parent's genetic make-up will be present in the offspring. Therefore, parents who have a favorable genetic endowment will have a high probability of producing children with a favorable genetic make-up. On the other hand, parents whose genetic endowment does not suit them for survival in the environment will not only produce fewer offspring on the average, they will also be less capable of caring for the offspring they produce. Furthermore, those offspring that survive inherit the less fit genetic make-up of the parent. The end result is clear; in the long run, the more fit survive and flourish, whereas the less fit wane and perish. However, it is not the more fit individual who survives; it is the most fit hereditary constitution that survives. It does so by making more copies that have a higher probability of copying themselves than less fit hereditary blueprints are able to produce. The process is completely automatic and impersonal. The fittest individuals are not necessarily the best fighters or the most aggressive, they are merely those who are constructed in such a fashion that they tend to have a higher probability of reproducing and rearing their young to reproductive age. This ability has been determined by their genetic inheritance.

An example borrowed from the noted ecologist Robert MacArthur might be of help. Let us suppose that you have two savings accounts: one pays interest at the rate of 4 per cent per year, and the other pays interest at 2 per cent per year. Let us suppose further that you deposit $100 in silver money into the 4 per cent account and the $100 in paper money into the 2 per cent account. Suppose also that the bank, for reasons of its own, pays the interest on the silver you have deposited with silver and interest on the paper you have deposited with paper. Finally, suppose that you make small withdrawals of $5 or $10 every six or seven months from the paper account. The silver, earning an interest of 4 per cent, which is twice as great, might be said to reproduce silver faster than the paper reproduces itself. Furthermore, because you make larger and more frequent withdrawals from the paper account than you do from the silver account, fewer of the paper dollars survive to a reproductive age (that time during the year when the bank pays interest) than do the silver dollars. These considerations hold not only for the initial deposits in silver and paper but for the silver offspring and the paper offspring. The results of such a situation are predictable. In the environment we have described, silver is more fit than paper. It is more fit because it reproduces more rapidly and it has a higher probability of reaching reproductive age. Our savings accounts will evolve in such a fashion that silver will become dominant and paper extinct. This will happen, not because silver and paper have engaged in some titanic battle with each other, but because of the differential rates of what might be loosely called reproduction and mortality.

In biological systems less fit genes tend to be eliminated through the operation of natural selection. This process, which results in the selection of one genotype[1] over another, is a reality that we encounter almost daily. Everyone is familiar with the kind of evolution that is fostered by man acting as nature's agent. Selection is imposed by the plant or animal breeder when he wants to produce a particular type of organism. The American Beauty rose and the dachshund are both the result of deliberate selection. A thousand years ago there were neither dachshunds nor American Beauty roses. These varieties of living things have evolved in the relatively recent past as a result of man's conscious effort and selection; in one case for a large thorny bush that produces fragrant blossoms with rich red petals, and in the other for an absurd little dog with short legs and a body like a sausage. These two examples, which find parallels in almost all our food plants and domestic animals, clearly demonstrate evolution under conditions of deliberate and conscious selection.

We can also observe evolution under natural conditions. In England there is a moth known as the peppered moth. Two color variations of this moth have been found, white and black. Until the middle of the nineteenth century, collectors reported finding only the white variety. However, black variants of the peppered moth have been found with ever greater frequency since 1850. The increase in the proportion of black moths has paralleled the growth of heavy smoke producing industries in England. As smoke polluted the atmosphere and surrounding countryside, roosting places for the peppered moth, such as trees and rocks, became black in color from the accumulation of soot particles. Today in and around these heavily industrialized sections we find a population of almost exclusively black peppered moths. But in those parts of the English countryside far from centers of industrial pollutants, we still find, as in the preindustrial period, that the white peppered moth predominates.

How do we explain the rapid rise in the population of black peppered moths and their association with industrial areas? It turns out that birds are fond of eating peppered moths — when they can find them. As with so many other animals, color in the peppered moth can be used as a means of camouflage. As shown in Figure 5-1, the white peppered moth alighting on a lichen-covered tree trunk in the unpolluted countryside is nearly invisible; however, the pigmented variety of this moth stands out in bold relief. Near an industrial area where many of the moth's roosting places have been

[1] Genotype — hereditary make-up.

Figure 5-1
Left, white and black peppered moths on a lichen-covered tree trunk. Right, white and black peppered moths on a soot-blackened tree trunk. (Photos from the experiments of Dr. H. B. D. Kettlewell, Oxford University)

covered with black soot, the situation is reversed. Here the dark-colored moths are almost invisible as they roost on soot-blackened backgrounds. Two factors, the eating habits of birds and industrial pollution, have combined to act as agents of natural selection to produce the evolution of a new variety of moth. This example of evolution involving color adaptation, called industrial melanism, has been observed in more than seventy different species of moths. Taken together these examples of industrial melanism constitute one of the most striking illustrations of rapid evolution that we know of.

Like the moth, man too is a product of evolution. The broad outlines of his evolutionary ascent can be obtained through a study of human and human-like fossils. Fossils are the remains in the form of bones or impressions of once-living organisms. They record the history of the three billion or so years of life on earth. Fossils from rock layers of different ages show a clear progression from simple to complex life forms. The earliest known fossils, which are more than three billion years old, show only bacteria, which are simple and primitive organisms. The most recent fossils, those of the past several million years, contain in addition to simple organisms the remains of large complex plants and animals. The ages of the rock formations in which fossils are embedded—and hence the age of the fossils themselves—can be determined by geologic techniques or by the application of radioisotope dating methods. It is through a study of the fossil record that we have come to know that one hundred million years ago dinosaurs were in New York City and dragonflies the size of hawks lived in Pennsylvania. The fossil record has been used to build the chart in Figure 5-2, which summarizes the three billion year history of life on earth.

One part of that history becomes distinguishable with the origin of the primates about 70 to 100 million years ago. Today the primate order contains such diverse creatures as tree shrews, lemurs, monkeys, apes, and men. This great group had its origin when its early ancestors evolved from small, insect-eating, ground-dwelling animals known as insectivores. The separation of the primates involved their adaption to an omnivorous, tree-dwelling mode of existence. The ascent of the primates into the trees led to the development of two key adaptations: the grasping hand and stereoscopic vision. The development of a hand with a thumb made primates the most successful and efficient of the tree-dwelling mammals. The development of stereoscopic vision, or depth perception, the ability to see in three dimensions, is a result of the forward movement of the eyes in the primate group. In other mammals the eyes are placed on either side of the head. Although this allows a wide field of vision for each eye, it permits little overlap of visual fields. Stereoscopic vision requires that the visual fields of both eyes overlap. The greater the overlap, the better the depth perception. Primate evolution is characterized by a flattening of the face and a progressive forward movement of the eyes. Both these evolutionary developments were selected by the new fitness requirements imposed by an arboreal way of life. High in the trees a good grasp and good depth perception had clear survival value. As the evolutionist McAlester has pointed out, these adaptations of hand and vision that arose in the trees proved to be of determinative

Figure 5-2
*Summary of life
on earth.*

Geologic Era	Millions of Years Ago	Geologic Epoch	First Appearance of the Indicated Life Form
Cenezoic	2.5	Pleistocene	Man
Cenezoic	7	Pliocene	Chimpanzees, Gorillas, Australopithecines
Cenezoic	26	Miocene	Apes
Cenezoic	38	Oligocene	Monkeys
Cenezoic	54	Eocene	Whales, Porpoises
Cenezoic	65	Paleocene	Primates
Mesozoic	136	Cretaceous	Mammals
Mesozoic	190	Jurassic	Flowering plants
Mesozoic	225	Triassic	Birds
Paleozoic	280	Permian	Gymnosperms
Paleozoic	325	Pennsylvanian	Reptiles
Paleozoic	345	Mississippian	
Paleozoic	395	Devonian	Amphibians
Paleozoic			Insects
Paleozoic	430	Silurian	Land plants
Paleozoic			Fishes
Paleozoic	500	Ordovician	Algae
Paleozoic	570	Cambrian	All major invertebrate phyla
Precambrian	2700		Oldest known green plants—algae
Precambrian	3100		Oldest known bacteria
Precambrian	3400		Origin of life
	4600		

Formation of the earth's crust

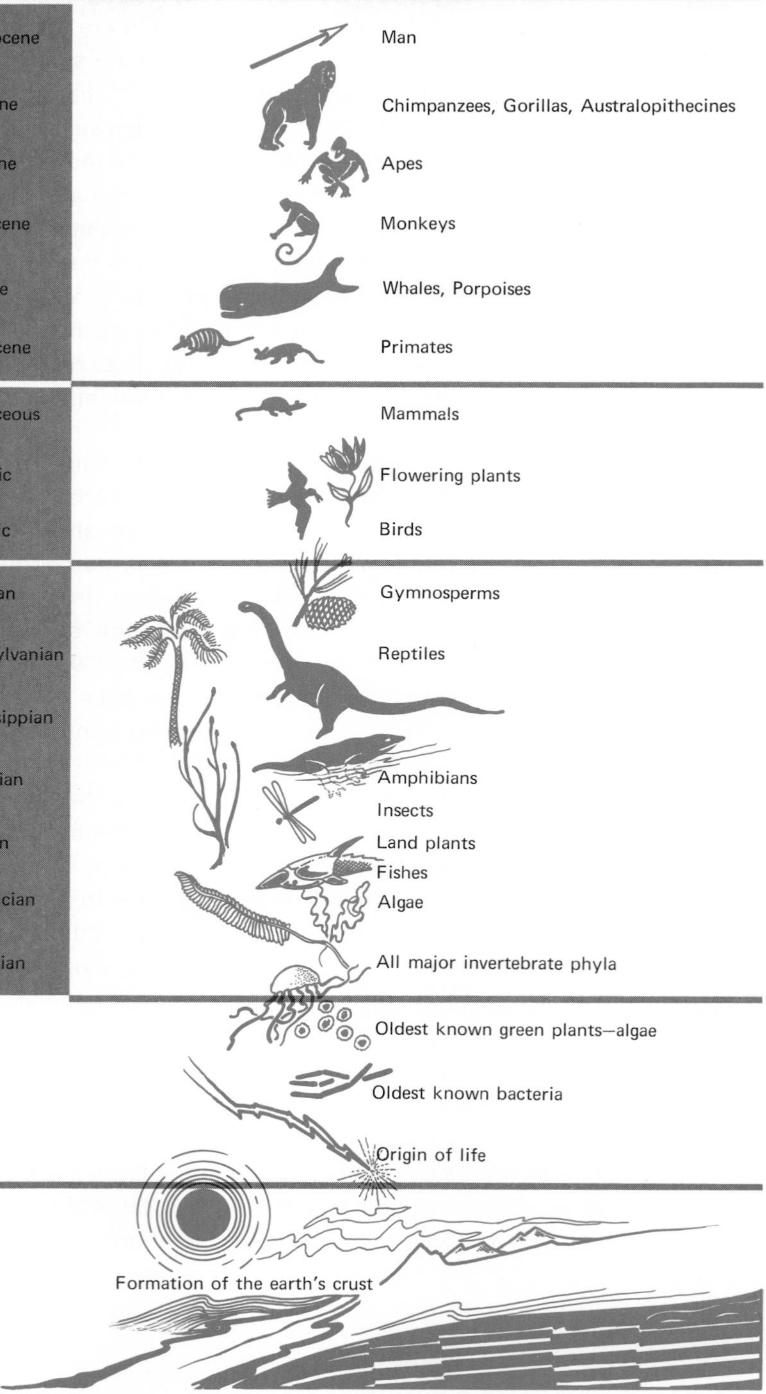

importance to the success of man on the ground. They enabled him to grasp tools and weapons and to coordinate mind, hand, and eye in such highly three-dimensional activities as tool making and hunting.

By 30 to 50 million years ago, the primate line had split to form branches that would become the monkeys and apes. In the evolution of the apes, a family type known as *Proconsul* (or *Dryopithecus*) marks a crossroads. From this stock there arose the apes of today: the gorilla, the chimpanzee, and the orangutan. It is also from this stock that we trace the ancestors of man.

Proconsul is linked to the first clearly distinguishable ape-like men through the transitional form, *Ramapithecus,* who lived about ten million years ago. *Ramapithecus,* whose few fossil fragments have been found in India and Africa, was a ground-dwelling ape whose dental pattern suggests a diet similar to that of later ape-men.

By two million years ago, *Ramapithecus* had given rise to the Australopithecines, ape-men that are clearly ancestral to ourselves. Skulls and limb bones of these early men have been found mostly in Africa, particularly in the Olduvai Gorge, a remote part of Tanzania. From the numerous remains of these early ape-men we can construct the following picture: They were of two sizes, one about that of a chimpanzee and the other a little larger. Both forms walked upright and by present-day standards had relatively large jaws. This upright carriage freed their hands for exploration of the environment, tool making, and the wielding of weapons. Stone implements of their construction are found with their fossils. Even though these implements are crude and rudimentary, the fractured skulls of baboons and other animals found on the campsites suggest that they were effective. Clearly, the use of tools enabled these ape-men to hunt and forage more effectively.

However, it is the production of tools, more than their use, that clearly set these early men and their descendants apart from the apes. Chimpanzees have been observed to use materials in their environment to accomplish a particular task. They will, for instance, use appropriately shaped sticks or stones to pry the bark off trees or dig up ant hills in order to get at the enclosed ants. However, under natural conditions, neither chimps nor any other apes use tools to make tools.

The Australopithecines are clearly in our ancestoral past, but they were so sufficiently different from modern man that we would have no difficulty distinguishing them. Some were short in stature, and they walked differently; the bone structure of their legs and pelvis did not accommodate the long, striding gait we practice. Their walk would have been closer to the rambling, shuffling trot characteristic of the apes. Even though these early men might have developed some primitive forms of speech, gross considerations of brain size suggest that they would not have had the mental capacity to carry out the kind of abstract and quantitative thought of which all varieties of modern men are capable. Examination of fossil skulls shows that the brain of the Australopithecine was much smaller than ours. We have a brain whose volume averages around 1,300 to 1,400 cc (almost a quart and a half). Studies of the skulls of these ape-men show that the volume of their brain was not much larger than 600 cc (a little more than a pint). Also, the shape of their heads indicates that there was not the extraordinary development of the frontal lobes (centers for abstract thought) for which we find accommodation in the higher-browed forehead of modern man.

From the Australopithecines the next and more advanced stage of human evolution developed. Because fossil remains of this stage have been found in many parts of Asia and in both North and South Africa, we can conclude that this early man was a wanderer. This next ancestor in the series of evolutionary steps leading to modern man appeared from 500,000 to 700,000 years ago and was similar in size to modern man. Because the bone development of his legs and feet was sufficiently like that of modern man to enable him to adopt the characteristic present-day posture and gait, we refer to this predecessor as *Homo erectus.* The study of his fossil remains demonstrates that as evolution was working toward a more efficient walking posture, it was also operating to select for a larger cranium that could accommodate a bigger and more powerful brain. *Homo erectus* had a brain capacity of around 1,000 cc (about a quart) almost twice that of the Australopithecines and more than two-thirds the average brain volume of modern man. His style of life reflected his greater intelligence.

He made a variety of tools, some of them relatively sophisticated. The layout of his caves indicates some evidence of social organization. He knew fire and exploited its potentialities for warming the caves in which he often dwelt, for warding off wild animals and for making some parts of his diet more palatable by cooking. Exploration of the caves of the variety of *Homo erectus* found in China (Pekin man) shows that his diet was varied. It included both meat and vegetables and, apparently, perhaps as a special delicacy, an occasional human brain and a scoop of human bone marrow. Pekin man's caves have revealed numbers of human skulls, neatly clipped off at the base as if to facilitate access to the contents, as well as a number of human long bones that have been cracked lengthwise to get at the marrow. Whether Pekin man limited his invitations for dinner to strangers or occasionally forced them on colleagues or even members of his own family is a matter for grisly speculation.

Homo erectus had his day. His wide geographical distribution and the fact that he left a number of fossils both indicate that, in his time, he was fairly successful. However, the development of man continued up the evolutionary road on which *Homo erectus* represented not an end but an advanced crossroad. From the ancestral stock of *Homo erectus* there arose, perhaps as long as 500,000 years ago, a new species of man (Figure 5-3). This form was *Homo sapiens,* our own species. He had a big brain, and he used fire, hunted skillfully, and made a variety of tools. But *Homo sapiens* was not only a tool maker; he was also an abstract thinker. Two of his early representatives, Cro-Magnon and Neanderthal man exercised this capacity in the practice of superstitious rites. For instance, the Neanderthal man buried his dead and often included with the corpse certain tools and artifacts he apparently believed the deceased would need in the next life. Cro-Magnon man made elaborate drawings of the animals he hunted. There are suggestions that these drawings related to some pattern of good-luck exercises in which the tribe indulged to secure the success of the hunt. The brain volume of both Cro-Magnon and Neanderthal suggests that either would have the intellectual capacity of contemporary man. Even though the short stature (about five feet), head shape, and massive shoulders of the Neanderthal man would make him recognizable in a group of contemporary men, this would not be true of the Cro-Magnon man. Cro-Magnon, an immediate ancestor of modern man, would be indistinguishable if he exchanged his cave man's garb for contemporary dress and strolled the downtown streets.

Whatever became of Neanderthal man? No one really knows. After thousands of years of coexistence with Cro-Magnon man he disappeared. Some students of evolution, aware of modern man's preference for eliminating competition by killing it off, have suggested that Cro-Magnon man was directly responsible for the extinction of the Neanderthals. Other students have suggested that the Neanderthal group was absorbed into the Cro-Magnon group by hybridization. In support of this view is the discovery of cave fossils that some scholars claim have a mixture of Neanderthal and Cro-Magnon characteristics. Perhaps a combination of intergroup warfare and intergroup hybridization is the answer to the disappearance of the Neanderthal. Perhaps other factors are primarily responsible. Certainly much more evidence is necessary before we can conclude the inquest into the mysterious disappearance of Mr. N.

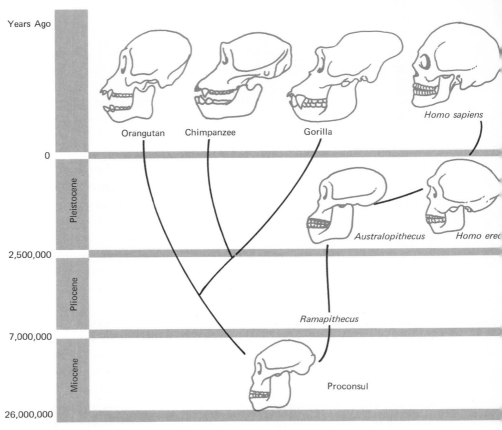

Years Ago

Orangutan   Chimpanzee   Gorilla   *Homo sapiens*

Pleistocene

Australopithecus   *Homo erec*

2,500,000

Pliocene

Ramapithecus

7,000,000

Miocene

Proconsul

26,000,000

Figure 5-3

Human evolution. Upper left: The ascent of man and the apes from a common ancestor, Proconsul. The evolution of skull structure as well as dental pattern is shown. Upper right: The rise of toolmaking. Lower left: Australopithecines foraging for food. Lower middle:

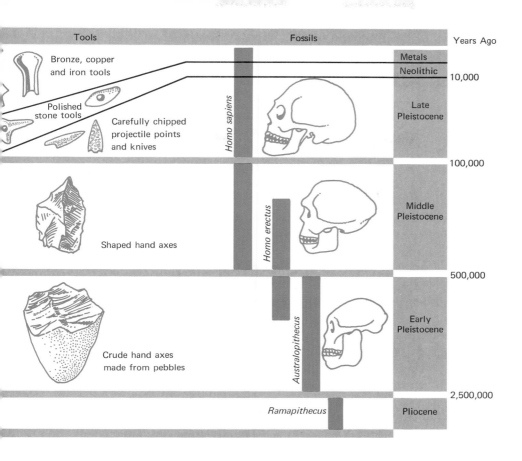

Tools	Fossils	Years Ago
Bronze, copper and iron tools	*Homo sapiens*	Metals
Polished stone tools		Neolithic — 10,000
Carefully chipped projectile points and knives		Late Pleistocene
		100,000
Shaped hand axes	*Homo erectus*	Middle Pleistocene
		500,000
Crude hand axes made from pebbles	*Australopithecus*	Early Pleistocene
		2,500,000
	Ramapithecus	Pliocene

Homo erectus, toolmaker with a sense of community. Lower right: Homo sapiens, an accomplished toolmaker who conceptualizes his environment. (Adapted from A. L. McAlester, The History of Life. *Englewood Cliffs, N.J.: Prentice-Hall, Inc., 1968.)*

The rigors of adapting to a changing or new environment required that men, like all other living things, adapt through evolution. Accordingly, the forces of natural selection have operated on man, as on all other biological systems, to produce a number of biological solutions to specific environmental problems. Biological evolution that resulted in a change in organic form was, as we shall see, one of the critical factors responsible for the development of these varieties of men we call races. In common with other living things, then, man too has traveled the branching road of organic evolution. But because he is, among living things, uniquely knowing and reasoning, he alone has been able to climb the ladder of cultural evolution.

Modern man is biologically clearly different from his ancestors. The biological difference that gave modern man, *Homo sapiens,* an advantage in controlling his environment over his immediate ancestor, *Homo erectus,* was his larger and more powerful brain. This biological difference has existed for hundreds of thousands of years. Because of his greater intelligence, *Homo sapiens* could cope more effectively with the demands of his environment. He could show greater foresight than *Homo erectus* in planning his activities, could organize more versatile and efficient hunts, and was probably capable of effecting a greater conceptualization of his environment. Consequently, he made better tools and arranged more complex community organizations than his ancestors, and slowly he began to increase his numbers (see Figure 5-4). These achievements would not have been possible without prior processes or organic evolution that culminated in the achievement of the larger brain of modern man. The crucial difference between the capacity of *Homo erectus* and early *Homo sapiens* to cope with their environments was organic, constitutional, and structural — that is to say, biological.

Now, compare the potential of a stone-age culture to control its environment and to divine the nature of its universe with that of a technological society of the 1970s. Because of the evolution of technology, at least 99 per cent of which has occurred during the past 500 years, a single individual equipped with materials he could buy for a year's salary could, left to himself, more greatly influence his environment in the course of a year than 1,000 members of a stone-age culture could have in the course of their lifetimes. Furthermore, his understanding of the workings of his universe and his stores of information are so great as to endow him with a relatively god-like knowledge and comprehension of his environment, compared with members of past, or even present, stone-age cultures. Contemporary man's power and omniscience are a result of his cultural evolution.

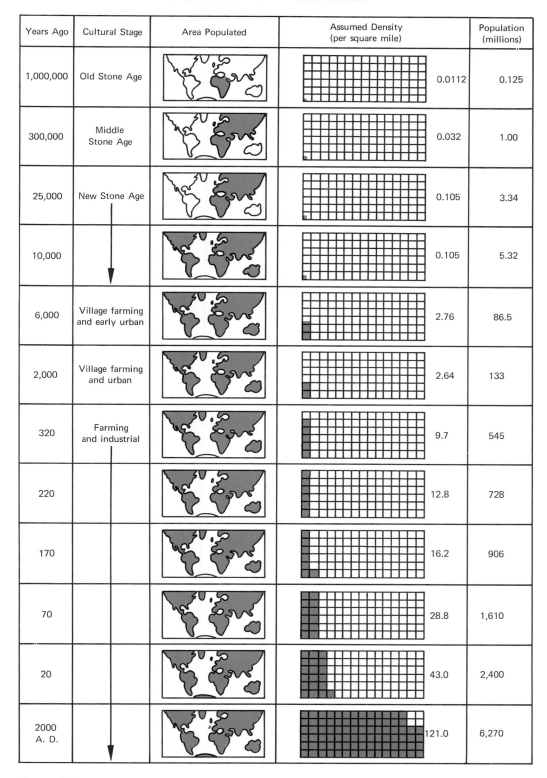

Years Ago	Cultural Stage	Area Populated	Assumed Density (per square mile)	Population (millions)
1,000,000	Old Stone Age		0.0112	0.125
300,000	Middle Stone Age		0.032	1.00
25,000	New Stone Age		0.105	3.34
10,000			0.105	5.32
6,000	Village farming and early urban		2.76	86.5
2,000	Village farming and urban		2.64	133
320	Farming and industrial		9.7	545
220			12.8	728
170			16.2	906
70			28.8	1,610
20			43.0	2,400
2000 A. D.			121.0	6,270

Figure 5-4

Past and projected growth of the human species. The introduction of agricultural practices less than 10,000 years ago has been followed by approximately a thousandfold increase in population.

Biological evolution depends on the passage of generations and, hence, time. A single individual cannot evolve biologically. Biological evolution is manifested by the future generations of a population of individuals. By its very nature it is a process that requires considerable time and is beyond the reach of a single individual.

Cultural evolution, on the other hand, is determined not so much by direct, temporal factors as by those of accumulation and exposure. First, the knowledge necessary to support a particular cultural mode must be accumulated somewhere. Secondly, individuals or populations must be exposed to this information. It is true that time is required to accumulate the knowledge necessary to evolve a particular cultural mode, but this time can be quite short when compared with the time required for profound biological evolution. Indeed, almost all the culture that represents the present-day mode of life has been evolved during the past 7,000 years and the technological culture that is the capstone of Western Civilization has evolved, as we saw earlier, during the past 500 years.

Unlike biological evolution, which of necessity requires generations, profound cultural evolution can take place within the lifetime of an individual or even the generation time of a population. Individuals living a tribal existence at a point of cultural development, perhaps comparable to that of Western Europe 3,000 years ago, can, with suitable education, take on the skills and many of the values of today's technologically evolved cultures. With appropriate education, an Eskimo can move from a hunting and gathering culture by way of the University of Alaska into a laboratory or a law office.

It is a fact of experience that all groups of men, irrespective of their biological diversity, appear to be capable, when they have the inclination and conditions are favorable, of taking on the cultural trappings of any other group. Japan, certainly not an industrial society as relatively recently as the early 1800s, has become just since then one of the world's industrial giants. The Chinese, also not an industrialized culture a hundred years ago, have put together with ominous alacrity an H-bomb and ballistic missiles. Zulus, who fought the Boers with spears, now fabricate steel and conduct chemical analyses; one of their number has won a Nobel Prize. Peace Corps volunteers from Brooklyn have successfully immersed themselves in tribal cultures quite different from the technological society in which they were reared. The Chinese American who lives in the Chinese section of San Francisco and works outside it speaks English during his working hours and functions in a cultural system that is typically American. After work he goes home, speaks Chinese, and often, quite deliberately, slips into a cultural system that is much closer to that of his ancestral home, China.

From these examples it is clear that men, because of their capacity for learning, are capable of enormous cultural plasticity. Men can and regularly do, when the circumstances are appropriate, successfully exchange one culture for another.

6

the origin of the races

One day the master potter decided it might be amusing to make men. So, he scooped up some clay, molded it into a man and put it into his kiln to bake. However, while it was baking something else attracted his attention, and he left it in the kiln too long. When he took it out, it had been blackened by the heat. Thus was born the black man. Realizing his mistake, the master potter fashioned another man and tried again. This time he took it out too soon, before it was fully baked, and thus was born the white man. Being a patient artisan, the master potter tried again. This time he was successful. There emerged from the kiln the perfectly formed, golden founder of the Chinese people.

[A Chinese folk tale]

And the sons of Noah that went forth of the ark was Shem, Ham, and Japeth. These are the three sons of Noah and of them was the whole earth overspread.

[A Judaic proclamation of the common origin of man, taken from the Old Testament (Genesis 9:18, 19)]

Color is the emblem of a curse visited by God on the sons of Ham. As the curse is lifted the hue lightens. Thus the black man still bears the full weight of the original curse.

[An explanation of skin color once advanced by the Mormon church]

These excerpts from the folk culture of different peoples testify to man's desire to understand why some men are one color and some another. They are an effort to explain how races came to exist. Like this folklore, our own discussion of human racial origins must be speculation too. The fossil record, so helpful in tracing man's descent from distant ancestors, cannot be used to verify our tentative conclusions.

Difficulties in interpretation prevent us from using the fossil record to gain information on the origin of contemporary human races. The anthropologist sometimes encounters difficulties in making a rigorous differentiation between fossils of *Homo erectus* and *Homo sapiens*, two different species of man separated in time. One of the most important characteristics on which to base this distinction is brain size—a generalization that remains true although complicated by the fact that there is some overlap in size between the larger cranial fossils left by *Homo erectus* and some of the smaller skulls found in populations of *Homo sapiens*. So, even where marked differences in populations exist, it can be difficult sometimes to separate the fossils of one group unequivocally from those of the other. Consider also the fact that the most magnificent fossils are, at best, only heaps of once interconnected bones. There is no hair, no skin, no flesh, and no blood. No amount of careful study of even the most perfect human fossils is going to allow one to determine whether the bones belonged to a black man with type O blood or to a white man with type A, Rh-negative blood. For these reasons we cannot go back into the fossil record and attach meaningful racial tags to the fossils of *Homo sapiens* that we examine. Added to this is the consideration that in order to establish a pattern of origin for a particular race, we would have to be able to see a gradation in time of racial characteristics that would culminate in one of today's existing racial types. To be useful in tracing racial origins the fossil record would be required to show not only clear racial differences but also the small and subtle divergence in time of group differences during the evolutionary ascent of a race. It can do neither.

Even though we are without the help of the fossil record, the definition of race that we arrived at earlier allows us to discuss the problem within the framework of biology. Recall that *a race is a breeding population characterized by certain gene frequencies that are different from other breeding populations of the same species.* The question of race formation and race maintenance now requires an understanding of what is necessary to establish and maintain differential gene frequencies in different populations.

Model Systems for Race Formation

Often in biology a problem of interest arises in a system so complex or so filled with unknowns that the path to solution is unclear or impassable. In these cases it is often useful to raise the question in a system that is simpler, better understood, and more easily studied. Such systems are called model systems. The intensive and rigorous study of a relatively few model systems has led to the discovery of a number of important principles that are generally relevant to all living organisms. Much of our current understanding of genetic processes in humans has come from investigations of heredity in such model systems as the fruit fly, the mold, and the bacterium. To clarify the basic factors responsible for race formation and the rate at which they can operate, we must turn to not one but two model systems. The first is provided by the conscious efforts of the plant breeder to develop new and desirable varieties of plants. The second comes from observations of the rate of race formation in the wild. Race formation in the sparrow population provides this natural model system.

The essential conditions for race formation and maintenance are regularly arranged by the plant breeder. Suppose he wanted to develop a race of an appropriate plant species that would have long stems and blue flowers. His method would require three critical steps: First, among existing populations he would watch for plants that were tall and also for plants that produced blue flowers. That is, he would use as a basic raw material for his molding of the new race those small but ever-present natural variations from the norm that occur in all populations of living organisms. Next he would mate the plants that had blue flowers with the tall plants. He would watch their offspring for an occasional type that represented a combination of the tall character of one parent and the flower color of the other parent. If his efforts were blessed with success, he would very deliberately select the seeds from this desired combination and plant them in an isolated tray or part of the garden. By doing this he would prevent crosses between his selected variety and other variety and other types. Upon the variant population that had been reared in genetic isolation he would again exercise selection for those plants that were tall and had blue flowers, crossing the desired types with each other. By application of this process of selection during a number of generations under conditions of genetic isolation, he would produce a new race of plants, bred to specifications.

His development of this race initially required the selection of natural variants and the offspring of natural variants having desirable properties. Then it depended on his ability to rear and mate these plants in genetic isolation. All these considerations — (1) variation, (2) selection, and (3) isolation — are of crucial importance in race formation.

Without the occurrence of natural variations in populations, the raw material for the selection of new lines does not exist, and evolution is precluded. Then some selection mechanism must operate to provide a relative increase in the production of one type over the other or the occasional variants will not necessarily increase their numbers any more rapidly than the parent population. In addition, genetic isolation is necessary to prevent the new variants from being absorbed back into the original population.[1] For example, it would not be possible to maintain a pure line of one variety of marigold if one grew it in a field of other types of marigolds in a manner that allowed free mating between the variant and the other marigold populations. Through a combination of absolutely rigorous selection and total genetic isolation, the plant breeder is able to produce in a few generations a variety of marigold that is genetically of one type — that is, a pure race of marigold. In the case of

---

[1] Later, in the section dealing with genetic drift we shall see that genetic isolation alone can sometimes act as a selective mechanism.

natural populations in which natural, rather than artificial, selection and isolation are the agents of evolution, one cannot expect to approach regularly the degree of racial purity that can be obtained by the patient and determined animal or plant breeder. In nature, instead of maintaining a 100 per cent frequency of the genes that used to characterize a racial population, one sees the maintenance of relatively high frequencies of certain characteristic genes or groups of genes. This is because in natural racial populations one finds a lack of total genetic isolation or a lack of absolute selection or a combination of both. Because in nature there are often exchanges of genes between different racial populations, total genetic isolation is not the rule. Absolute selection is usually absent also, because often a particular racial characteristic will confer only a slight advantage in a particular natural environment rather than an absolute advantage. Hence, those atypical individuals in the population who arise through natural variation or who have inherited genes from other races as a result of imperfect isolation are not rigorously pruned by the forces of natural selection. Because these conditions apply to an extreme degree in human populations, there are no pure races of man. The extraordinary and overlapping variations within the races of man represent indisputable proof of their lack of purity and their highly hybrid nature.

Given the inefficiency of race formation when neither selection nor isolation is absolute, just how many generations might be necessary for the differentiation of a parent population into clearly recognizable racial varieties? The answer comes from studies of race formation in the house sparrow. The founding population of sparrows was introduced into America in 1852. From an East Coast zone of entry, succeeding generations have spread west to California, south into Mexico, and north into Canada. Populations of sparrows can now be found in damp coastal areas of Louisiana and in the dry, hot deserts of Arizona. They thrive on the cold northern plains of central Canada and in the heat of Houston, Texas. Today, one can demonstrate that different geographical populations of sparrows show characteristic differences in color, wing length, bill length, and body weight. Using these differences as guides, more than a dozen racial varieties of sparrows can be clearly identified. Distance serves, substantially, even if not perfectly, to isolate breeding populations of sparrows from each other. Environmental factors — particularly climate — provide strong, although not absolute, selection pressure. For example, it is known that there is a relationship between optimal body size and climate. Cold climates tend to select for a heavier, heat-conserving body that minimizes the surface-to-volume ratio. Table 6-1 shows that precisely this relationship holds

Locality	Average Body Weight (grams)
Houston, Texas	28.0
Austin, Texas	28.0
Los Angeles, California	28.2
Salt Lake City, Utah	28.7
Lawrence, Kansas	29.4
Montreal, Quebec	30.4
Edmonton, Alberta	30.8

Table 6-1.
Geography and Body Weight in Racial Populations of House Sparrows

After Eugene Schreider, "Ecological Rules, Body-Heat Regulation, and Human Evolution, in *Evolution*, **18**(1964).

for sparrows taken at a variety of locations. Those from cold regions like Edmonton, Alberta, are the heaviest. Those from climates like Texas and California are the lightest. Samples from climates between these extremes have intermediate values.

Before the results of this study were published a few years ago, evolutionary theorists assumed that more than 1,000 generations would be necessary for racial differentiation in birds. The discovery that all these races of sparrows evolved within one hundred generations came as a bombshell. It is clear that in nature evolution at the racial level can be extremely rapid. In a human population one hundred generations cover a timespan of about 2,000 years. These studies suggest that given a reasonable degree of isolation and strong selection pressure, relatively short periods may be required for the elaboration of some racial characteristics in man.

Race Formation in Man

Race-related differences seen in human populations are not merely curiosities, thoughtfully arranged by the Creator for the amusement of anthropologists. Many of the structural and constitutional features associated with race represent, in common with other biological structures, an adaptation to the environment made by the organism at some stage during its evolution. Color, certain aspects of blood chemistry, body structure, and physiology can all be viewed as biological adaptations. These adaptations demonstrate the capacity of man, like all other living things, to respond biologically to environmental challenges. Given genetic isolation, the pressure of a selective environment, and the passage of generations, populations will shift toward a higher frequency of adaptive genes. Since his emergence, man has invaded vastly different areas of the world. We are certain that in his early, relatively precultural, days his biological adaptability was of considerable importance in his successful occupation of new areas. Many of the characteristics, some of which we shall examine, associated with racial groups represent a collection of solutions to environmental challenges buried in the history of the population. This does not mean that *every* racial characteristic can claim to have had at some time a crucial or even a significant function in the survival of the population. Passenger traits, nonpaying but that just happen to be along for the ride, can be included by chance. It is possible that some racial traits like the shoveled incisors of Mongoloid populations or the blue penises of some South American Indians, although significant for racial characterization, are insignificant for survival. The operation of genetic drift,[2] a sort of random selection, may account for the chance inclusion of some of the passenger traits that mark racial populations. But before considering the possible role played by drift in race formation, we should examine those racial characteristics that are adaptive.

Color

Few factors are as important in determining the selection pressures of an environment as the quantity and quality of sunlight it receives. Solar intensity varies with latitude, being highest around the equator and diminishing as one moves out of the tropics toward the poles. At any time of the year the amount of sunlight a particular environment receives is fixed. Therefore it is a given to which all populations in a particular environment must accommodate. Human populations are not exempted from the necessity of accommodation.

The amount of sunlight an individual productively absorbs has a profound influence on his nutrition and health. Skin color, which can vary in populations, provides a means of regulating the amount of sunlight productively absorbed. For reasons that will become apparent, it is quite possible that a failure to regulate properly the productive absorption of sunlight can have lethal consequences. Thus, one would expect that an environmentally appropriate skin color would be favored by the most powerful of selective pressures.

Primarily, it is what we know about vitamin D and the role of sunlight in its production that leads us to emphasize the importance of skin color. Vitamin D maintains proper calcium metabolism. Severe disease results when there is too much or too little vitamin D. Too little vitamin D results in an inadequate deposition of calcium

---

[2] See later discussion of genetic drift.

and the bones soften. Rickets, characterized by extremely bowed legs and twisted spines, is the disease of vitamin D deficiency. Too much vitamin D results in the overdeposition of calcium. This causes extremely brittle, and thus easily broken, bones as well as large depositions of calcium in parts of the body where it is harmful (kidney stones, for example).

Until very recently man depended on his own body chemistry and the sun to produce just the amount of vitamin D he needed. Vitamin D is synthesized in a layer of cells just under the skin when they are illuminated with ultraviolet light from the sun. This is why vitamin D is known as the sunshine vitamin. Because most foodstuffs contain negligible amounts of vitamin D, diet is not an important source (see Table 6-2). Therefore in a state of nature where there are no bottles of fish liver oils or cartons of vitamin D-enriched milk, you must make it for yourself.

One's ability to make it in the proper amounts depends on the ability of the activating light of the sun to penetrate the outer layer of skin and reach the underlayer of cells that is capable of using this light to produce vitamin D. If the sunlight is dim and the skin is dark, little of this energy source necessary for the production of this indispensable vitamin can penetrate and the individual will not make enough to meet the requirements of his system. On the other hand, if the sunlight is intense and the skin is very fair, then too much ultraviolet light will reach the vitamin D-synthesis layer and an overproduction will result. So, in the state of nature, natural selection will favor those individuals whose coloration best enables them to use the available sunlight to produce enough, but not too much, vitamin D. At latitudes as far north as London the sunlight is pale and much less intense than at locations in the tropics. The pale, thin, fair skin of the Swede is magnificently adapted to filter out as little as possible of the weak sunlight that is characteristic of the northern latitudes. Indeed, an area of white skin comparable to that comprising the cheeks of a baby admits enough light to produce something

Source	Vitamin D Units per Ounce
Milk (unenriched for vitamin D)	3.2
Butter	12.8
Cream	16.0
Egg yolk	160.0
Calf liver	0.0
Olive oil	0.0
Codliver oil	1,920–9,600
Halibut liver oil	64,000–128,000

Table 6-2.
Natural Sources of Vitamin D

Adapted from Coward's *The Biological Standardization of the Vitamins* (Baltimore: Wood, 1938), p. 223.

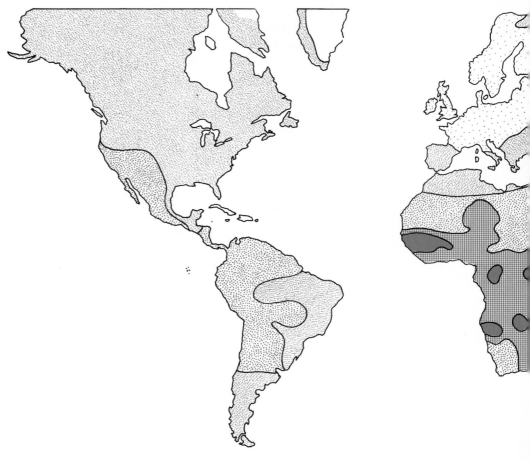

Figure 6-1

Distribution of skin color prior to 1492. (Adapted from C. L. Brace and M. F. A. Montagu, Man's Evolution. *New York: Macmillan, 1965.)*

like 400 units of vitamin D. This is equivalent to the minimum daily requirement. The heavily pigmented skin of the Black is so impermeable to sunlight that even if a larger area of his body were exposed to the pale northern rays, he could not synthesize the minimum daily requirement of vitamin D.

In the tropics conditions are reversed. Without the benefit of cultural devices such as proper clothing and appropriately designed dwellings, the pale-skinned northerner would be ill-suited for survival under the brilliant equatorial sun of the tropics. His transparent skin passes too much ultraviolet radiation. Consequently he produces too much vitamin D and suffers the toxic effects of this overabundance.

○ Lightest
◍ Medium light
◒ Medium
◍ Medium dark
● Darkest

Because the synthesis of vitamin D must be in an amount that is not too much and not too little, but just right—the Goldilocks condition—it was most probably a crucial factor in racial differentiation. Man arose in the warm, sunny even climates of Africa and Asia. He later spread into the northern latitudes of Asia and throughout Europe. He thus came to occupy a number of environments where the sun was less intense than in the cradling homelands. These movements, and consequently the adjustments to the new environments, took place in a relatively precultural period of man's history. Thus we expect that many of his adjustments to the new environments had to be constitutional rather than technological. In this long-past, precultural period of man's early history, human populations experienced a powerful selection for appropriateness of skin color. The distribution of skin color as a function of latitude is depicted on the map in Figure 6-l. This map of color distribution in human populations prior to the voyages of discovery in 1492 supports the suggestion that skin color is an adaption to sunlight.

It is clear that dark skins are not the exclusive possession of the Negro races. Progressively darker skins as one approaches the tropics are also found in Mongoloid, Caucasoid, Indian, and Australoid populations.

Adaptation to Cold and to Heat

Different populations of man show different constitutional adaptations to temperature. These are expressed in body form, circulatory patterns, basal metabolic rates, and group differences in tolerance to heat stress.

One of the most powerful environmental stresses men have faced is cold. Body architecture is an adaption of crucial importance. A thin, gangling body with a high surface-to-mass ratio is ill-adapted to conserve heat. A heavy body with short arms and legs is much better adapted; it exposes far less surface and consequently loses less heat to the surroundings. But the body structure must not only conserve body heat; those portions of the anatomy, the hands and the face, that must function even when they are exposed to the cold should be appropriately designed. A flat face with low nasal silhouette, narrow eye slits, and a padding of insulating fat would serve its bearer well in the cold. The Eskimos are biologically as well as culturally adapted for survival in the Arctic cold. Collectively, they form a group that embodies all the cold adaptations we have mentioned. Figure 6-2 shows how beautifully the Eskimo body is adapted to retain heat. We can conclude this discussion of cold adaptation by noting that hands which must maintain dexterity should receive an increased supply of warming blood when they are stimulated by cold. Some studies have indicated that after stimulation by exposure to cold, there is a greater increase of blood flow in the hands of Eskimos and other Mongoloid populations than in the hands of other races.

The human body had to make an equally effective adaptation to extremes of heat. Here a lean body with long heat-exchanging extremities is a highly desirable model. The Negro body type with its relatively short body and long limbs represents a body build adapted to lose heat (see Figure 6-3). In addition to this body type found with high frequency in Black populations, some studies have suggested other physiological differences in heat tolerance. Blacks appear to show a greater tolerance for humid heat than other groups. The parallel observation that American Black soldiers suffered more cold-related injuries in the Korean War than Whites would argue by contrast for heat adaptation in the Black.

Figure 6-2
*A group of Green-
land Eskimos.*

Peabody Museum, Harvard
University

Figure 6-3
*A Zulu mother
and child.*

Peabody Museum, Harvard University

Throughout the world, malaria kills more of mankind than any other infectious disease. This often fatal affliction, characterized by chills and fever, is caused by the single-celled microscopic parasite *Plasmodium falciparum* and its relatives. This disease-producing microorganism, which is spread from person to person by mosquitoes, lives and multiplies in the red blood cells of its host. The degree to which the malaria parasite thrives in the bloodstream of an infected individual depends on the structure of the hemoglobin in the red blood cell. The structure of hemoglobin, a large protein molecule that carries oxygen from the lungs to the tissues, is genetically determined. Most individuals have genes for the production of normal hemoglobin. However, some people possess genes that direct the production of abnormal hemoglobins. For reasons not thoroughly understood, the malaria parasite multiplies less rapidly in the red blood cells of individuals with appropriately abnormal hemoglobins. Consequently, those who have genes for the production of malaria-resistant modifications of hemoglobins suffer a milder and less fatal malarial infection than individuals with completely normal hemoglobin.

The operation of natural selection is such that in areas where malaria is prevalent we find a high frequency of individuals carrying genes for hemoglobins with malaria-resistant modifications. Populations carrying a high frequency of genes for antimalarial hemoglobins pay a price for their protective adaptation. In two well-known diseases associated with malaria-resistant modifications, thalassemia and sickle-cell anemia, abnormal hemoglobins are produced. These variant hemoglobins have an impaired capacity for oxygen transport. In the case of sickle-cell anemia, the abnormal hemoglobin molecules tend to coagulate in the red blood cells causing them to adopt a shrunken, sickle-like shape (see Figure 6-4). Thalassemia is characterized by an overproduction of an immature form of hemoglobin. During the gestation period, the human embryo makes a form of hemoglobin called fetal hemoglobin, which is different from that found in adults. After birth the normal infant stops making fetal hemoglobin and switches over to production of mature hemoglobin. In acute thalassemia large amounts of fetal hemoglobin are produced throughout life. In sickle-cell anemia only the sickling type of hemoglobin is produced. Both of these diseases of the blood, which are fatal, are inherited. You will recall that in humans there are two copies of each of the genes, including those for hemoglobin production. When parents who are each heterozygous (they contain one normal hemoglobin gene and one defective gene) have children, they have one chance in four of producing a child that is homozygous (both genes are defective) for the hemoglobin defect (see Detail

Figure 6-4
Red blood cells from normal individuals (a), and individuals with sickle-cell anemia (b).

Diagram 3). The blood of homozygous carriers of sickling and of thalassemic traits fails to carry sufficient oxygen. Afflicted individuals rarely live to adulthood and therefore they do not reproduce. How, then, are genes so surely lethal in homozygous combination able to confer any selective advantage?

In a malarial area, a person who has the thalassemic or the sickling trait in a heterozygous form experiences a much milder and far less lethal form of malaria than those who do not carry the trait. Therefore, he is less likely to die from the disease during infancy or early childhood. And even though under certain conditions the individual who possesses these genes, even in heterozygous forms, may be somewhat weakened, in a malarial area, his possession of them makes it more probable that he will survive to reproductive age than the person with the normal genotype for hemoglobin. Hence, where malaria is common the advantages of the gene out-weigh the disadvantages, and the gene appears in a high proportion of populations who inhabit or have recently left areas of high mala-rial incidence. Once the population has left the area where malaria is prevalent, the frequency of the gene tends to decrease. Once outside the area of malaria prevalence, genes for sickling or thalas-semia have no adaptive advantage but they still may cause weaken-

Detail Diagram 3
The genetics of the antimalarial hemoglobins (see pages 98, 99).

One of the blood's primary functions is the transport of oxygen from the lungs to the tissues of the body. It is able to perform this important function because the red blood cells contain large amounts of hemoglobin. The structure of the hemoglobin molecule is such that it combines with oxygen in the lungs, where the oxygen is abundant, and releases it in the tissues, where oxygen concentration is much lower. The production of hemoglobin is controlled by two sets of genes, one set on each of two homologous chromosomes. You will recall that there are two of each type of chromosome present in each cell of an individual. The members of each pair are said to be homologous to each other and are spoken of as homologues. Any given set of hemoglobin genes on a particular homologue may dictate the production of a normal hemoglobin or, if the gene set is abnormal, an abnormal hemoglobin. Because an individual has two sets of genes for hemoglobin production, his genotype, or gene set, must be one of three types:

(A) Both sets specify the production of normal hemoglobin. Such an individual is said to carry the genes for the production of normal hemoglobin homozygously.

(B) One set is normal and the other set is abnormal. The genotype of these individuals is said to be heterozygous with respect to the genes for hemoglobin production.

(C) Both sets are abnormal. The genotype of these individuals is homozygous for the genes that produce abnormal hemoglobin.

The sickling trait with respect to genotypes and patterns of inheritance is as follows:

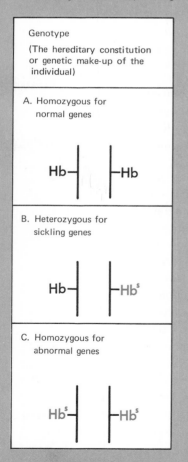

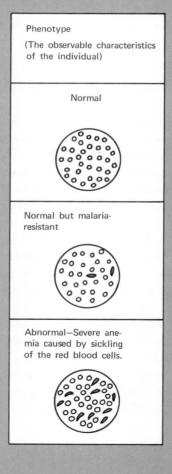

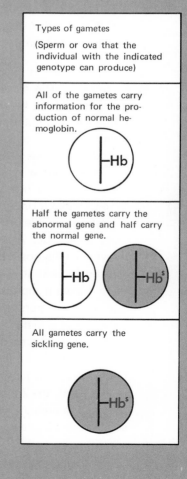

Genotype	Phenotype	Types of gametes
(The hereditary constitution or genetic make-up of the individual)	(The observable characteristics of the individual)	(Sperm or ova that the individual with the indicated genotype can produce)
A. Homozygous for normal genes	Normal	All of the gametes carry information for the production of normal hemoglobin.
B. Heterozygous for sickling genes	Normal but malaria-resistant	Half the gametes carry the abnormal gene and half carry the normal gene.
C. Homozygous for abnormal genes	Abnormal—Severe anemia caused by sickling of the red blood cells.	All gametes carry the sickling gene.

Hb A chromosome bearing genes for normal hemoglobin production.

Hb^s A chromosome bearing the gene for the abnormal hemoglobin, which is responsible for the sickling trait.

The characteristics of children expected to be produced by mating of:

1. Genotype A X Genotype A

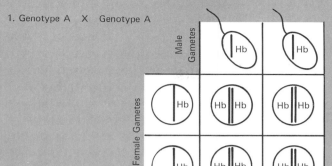

None of the offspring will be carriers of the sickling gene and none will have sickle cell anemia.

2. Genotype A X Genotype B

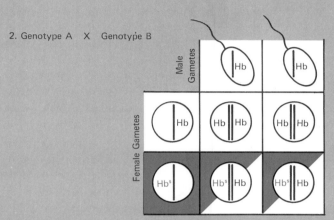

There is a 50 per cent probability that any child of such a mating will carry the sickling gene. None of the offspring will have sickle cell anemia. Matings between individuals heterozygous for the sickling trait with individuals who are homozygous for normal hemoglobin genes will not produce offspring with sickle cell anemia.

3. Genotype B X Genotype B

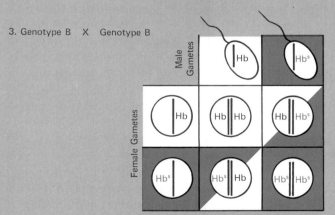

There is a 50 per cent probability that any given child of such a mating will carry the sickling cell but not have sickle cell anemia.

There is a 25 per cent probability that any given child of a mating between heterozygous carriers of the sickling gene will have sickle cell anemia.

4. Genotype C X Genotype C

The individuals are so weakened by their anemia that their probability of reproducing is small enough to be neglected.

Figure 6-5

Distribution of malaria and the antimalarial anemias. Upper left: The distribution of malaria in the Old World. Lower left: The distribution of thalassemia in the Old World. Upper right: The distribution of sickle-cell anemia. (Adapted from A. C. Allison, 1957.)

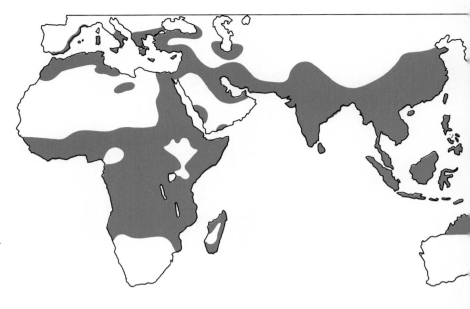

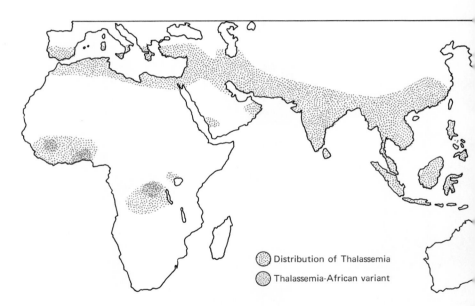

⬤ Distribution of Thalassemia

⬤ Thalassemia-African variant

ing. More importantly, whenever carriers of the gene mate, there is the possibility that the gene will be eliminated through formation of homozygotes. Because these homozygotes have a low probability of reproduction, in the absence of selection for the heterozygotes the frequency of such genes gradually decreases.

There is a clear coupling between the frequency of sickling and thalassemic genes and the geographical distribution of malaria.

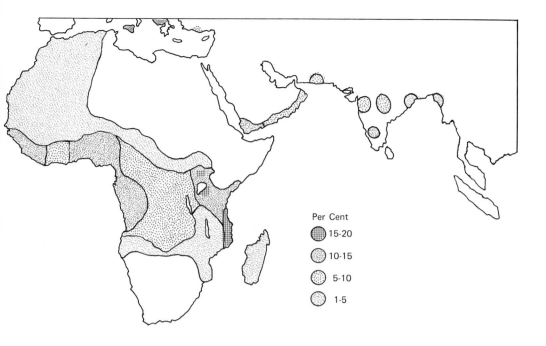

Per Cent
- ◉ 15-20
- ◉ 10-15
- ◉ 5-10
- ◉ 1-5

In areas of high malarial incidence, one finds a high proportion of such genes in the populations (see Figure 6-5). Thalassemia is found in malarial areas of Italy, Greece, some parts of Africa, Southern Asia, and New Guinea. Sickling, commonly found in Negro populations, is concentrated in West Africa, but it is also seen in East Africa. The sickling trait is found with decreasing frequency among Afro-Americans. Thalassemia is also much less frequent in populations of Italians and Greeks who immigrated to the New World from malarial regions of those countries. The decrease in the frequency of the abnormal hemoglobin traits in these populations is probably due to decreased adaptive value of thalassemia and sickling in the United States, where malaria is virtually nonexistent. One should also mention in concluding this discussion of a race-related adaptation to a common disease that in parts of Southeast Asia and Indonesia one finds another abnormal form of hemoglobin, hemoglobin-E; this form, in combination with thalassemic genes, acts to protect those populations against malaria.

Lactose
Intolerance: The
Interaction of
Culture and
Genetics to
Produce a Racial
Trait

Genetic theory forces the consideration of culture as the major factor in the evolution of man. . . . There is, then, no possibility of studying human raciation, the process of race formation, without studying human culture.
—S. L. Washburn

Milk is one of the closer approaches to the perfect food that we know. It contains an assortment of minerals, especially calcium, essential to health. It is a source of protein for tissue building and repair, and it contains two of the basic types of molecules—fats and carbohydrates—from which living organisms normally derive the energy necessary to support their activities. It is not surprising then that whatever the mammal—human, hamster, rabbit, or camel—nature has chosen milk as its first meal on birth into this world. Consequently, we would expect that all newborns, including the human infant, would possess the innate capacity to assimilate and thrive on the components of this primary dietary resource. This is indeed the case. All but a few human infants are able to digest and utilize the components of milk. However, in a few rare cases that often are accompanied by severe diarrhea, and even death, the newborn infant is unable to utilize lactose, the carbohydrate component of the milk that makes up most of its dry weight. But, as indicated, the failure of infants to tolerate lactose is rare. Thus, it was with some surprise that the scientific community greeted the announced results of a study, in 1965, in which Johns Hopkins University researchers had given lactose—milk sugar—to a large group of White and Black adult volunteers.

The researchers found that lactose intolerance, a mild but worrisome ailment in an adult who does not use milk as a sole source of nutrients, was reported by only 6 to 15 per cent of the White volunteers. However, after consuming 50 grams of lactose (about the amount present in a quart of milk), more than 70 per cent of the Blacks tested reported bloating, flatulence, and diarrhea—classic symptoms of lactose intolerance.

This finding suggested that different populations might differ dramatically in their tolerance to milk sugar and, by extension, to milk itself. A survey of many different populations the world over produced the findings sketched in Table 6-3. Clearly, in most of mankind, the ability to use milk sugar beyond early childhood is rare. Thus, we see that a little more than three quarters of the world's population, including the peoples of China, much of Africa and India, and Southeast Asia, are lactose intolerant. It is only in Europe and some pockets of Africa, India, and other parts of the world that we find lactose tolerance to be the rule.

Population	Percentage of Population Lactose Intolerant
Australian Aborigine	90
Greenland Eskimo	72
Chinese	83–97
Thai	87–100
East and South African Bantu	89–91
People of the Indian subcontinent*	63
Yoruba people of Nigeria	98–100
Ibo people of Nigeria	98–100
Swedish	3
Swiss	12
Finnish	17
United States Caucasoid	6–15
United States Black	70

Table 6-3.
Lactose Intolerance in Populations of the World

*India is a place of great cultural heterogeneity. In some regions of India, such as the Punjab, the highest milk producing area in the country, milk drinking is common, and we find that many of the individuals from that region are lactose tolerant. Also, if we take a look at the Sikhs, a religious group that has the highest milk consumption in all of India, we find that many individuals belonging to this group are lactose tolerant. On the other hand, if we look at those regions of the Indian subcontinent in which milk production is low, then we find the majority of these individuals are lactose intolerant.

Let us consider first the physiological basis of lactose intolerance and then inquire into the reasons why some populations are lactose tolerant and others are lactose intolerant. Before it can use milk sugar, the body must break it down into simpler sugars, one of which is glucose. This transformation of lactose into its readily absorbable and metabolically usable forms is accomplished by an enzyme called lactase, which is elaborated by certain regions of the walls of the small intestine. If the enzyme is present, most of the lactose taken in as a consequence of the consumption of milk, or many milk products such as ice cream, is digested to simpler sugars and absorbed by the intestine. On the other hand, if the lactase level is too low, the ingested milk sugar passes down into the lower intestine where it causes the absorption by the lower bowel of excess water from the surrounding tissues, which can result in a watery diarrhea. Furthermore, the microorganisms that inhabit the lower intestine feed on the lactose and produce, as a byproduct of their metabolism, excessive amounts of intestinal gas. The production of this excessive intestinal gas causes an uncomfortable feeling of bloating in the lactose intolerant subject, which often is accompanied by an irresistible but embarrassing flatulence.

What is the basis of this variation in the ability to handle milk sugar that we see between different human population groups? The most probable answer has been suggested independently by Robert D. McCracken and by Frederick J. Simoons, both of whom happen, by coincidence, to be affiliated with the University of California. They point out that lactose intolerance is seen in those human populations that do not have a history of dairying, whereas lactose tolerance is the rule in populations, such as those of Western Europe, that have had a cultural history that includes many hundreds of years of dairying. Their reasoning is as follows: The diet of dairying populations will include substantial quantities of milk. The capacity to utilize fully all of the energy potentially available from this food source would confer a selective advantage — small but quite important over many generations — on those individuals who possessed the hereditary capacity to utilize lactose in the postchildhood years. Consequently, the forces of natural selection, over the course of generations, would operate to increase the frequency of individuals who maintain the capacity to make lactase. As a result, we would expect to find that lactose tolerance is the rule in such populations. Inspection of Table 6-3 indicates that this is precisely the case. All of those populations listed in the table as having a low frequency of lactose intolerance come from populations that have a cultural history of dairying that reaches back into many tens or even hundreds of generations. Also, we find that in regions of the world where lactose intolerance is the rule, such as in many parts of Africa, there are isolated populations, such as the Masai of Kenya, that historically have included milk and its products as part of their diet. In these cases, we find that the isolated populations form islands of lactose tolerance in a sea of nondairying, nonmilk drinking, lactose-intolerant populations. Examination of the cultural patterns of countries such as China, Japan, Thailand, and many other parts of the world shows that these populations neither maintain large dairy herds nor consume milk. Furthermore, this has been true for hundreds or even thousands of years of their cultural history. Consequently, the rare individual who from time to time appeared in these populations and possessed the ability to produce lactase in the postchildhood years experienced no selective advantage. Consequently, the gene has remained rare in these populations.

If we look at the population of the United States we find that samples of many of the world's racial groups are represented. We find that substantial numbers of individuals in the United States, on the order of perhaps 20 per cent, or approximately 40 million people, are lactose intolerant. This rather sizable fraction of the population is composed of the majority of American Blacks, most Asian Americans and American Indians, a sizable fraction of the Puerto Rican and Mexican-American populations, and perhaps 10 per cent (about

17 million) of the Whites. Consideration of the large numbers of individuals here in the United States who are lactose intolerant has caused public health officials to wonder whether it might not be wise to make available milk products in which the lactose has been broken down into its simple sugar components during the course of processing. If such a course of action were taken, it would make available to those individuals who are lactose intolerant whole milk products from which they could derive the maximum nutritional benefit while avoiding the lactose-intolerant syndrome.

The phenomenon of lactose tolerance and lactose intolerance illustrates the role that cultural practices may play in the fixation of certain inherited traits in racial groups. Adoption of the cultural practice of dairying and the drinking of milk has fixed the maintenance of lactase throughout life in certain populations, particularly the Northwest European Caucasoids. However, most of the world's population is not milkdrinking and, hence, does not maintain within its gene pool large numbers of individuals who are lactose tolerant. Contrary to the advertisement that "Everybody Needs Milk," not everybody does.

Genetic Drift and Race Formation

Earlier we saw that not every racial trait has survival value. Many of the peculiarities of form and internal chemistry that identify racial populations cannot be shown to confer any biological advantage whatever. The spread of noses, the fullness of lips, the shoveling of incisors, the protrusion of ears, and the urinary excretion of BAIB are all indices that can be associated to a greater or lesser degree with racial types. Yet no one would strongly propose that they have increased their possessors' capacity to survive. Until now we have emphasized the role of natural selection in increasing the frequency of adaptive genes and decreasing the frequency of deleterious ones. This provided a neat and satisfying explanation for the different frequencies with which genes for skin color, body build, and anti-malarial hemoglobins occur in different human populations. At some time in the history of a population we proposed, adaptive forms of these genes made their holders more fit. The consistent contribution of more offspring to succeeding generations by the more fit individuals was eventually reflected in a higher frequency of these adaptive genes in the population.

But this does not explain the marked frequency differences with which neutral traits appear in different populations. Clearly, because the traits confer no advantage or disadvantage on the population, some mechanism other than selection through fitness is needed. In small populations, chance supplies that mechanism. When the pool of potential mates is small, chance mating or the chance removal of potential mates can cause an upward or downward drift of gene frequencies in that population. If this small population becomes the stem, or founding, population from which a large one grows, the different gene frequencies may be reflected in the emergent population.

A simple but extreme example will illustrate the operation of genetic drift. Consider a time 20,000 or 30,000 years ago when human populations were sparsely distributed collections of small tribes. Suppose a tribe of 45 members is made up of 20 adults and 25 children. Suppose, further, that 15 of the children carry the gene for high BAIB excretion and 10 do not. In this situation, 60 per cent of those children who will produce the next generation carry this gene and 40 per cent do not. Suppose a tiger surprised a group of these children at play and killed, just by chance, 5 children who do not carry the BAIB-excretion gene. The future generations of this tribe will now be drawn from a pool whose frequency is 75 per cent excretor gene–25 per cent nonexcretor gene. The gene frequency for BAIB excretion has suddenly drifted upward solely because some nonexcretors just happened to be in the wrong place at the right time. Any shifts in the frequency of adaptive or deleterious genes could be brought back into environmental harmony by the pressures of selection. However, because we have declared the BAIB-excretion genes neutral, they will not be affected by natural selection.

The founder principle can also act to establish new breeding populations with gene frequencies different from those of other populations. Suppose the hypothetical small tribe described here split into two factions and moved apart. Suppose also that one faction was largely composed of those who carried the excretor gene. Populations emerging from these two different stem, or founder, populations would differ sharply from each other with respect to the frequency of genes for BAIB excretion.

Hybrid Racial Populations

In addition to genetic drift and selection, interracial hybridization also provides a mechanism by which new breeding populations with characteristic gene frequencies can be established. Looking around the world, we can identify populations that are the result of the large-scale hybridization of two or more different breeding populations. Some of the largest of these hybrid populations can be found in the New World. Shortly after the voyages of Columbus, Spaniards invaded the Americas. Soon a pattern of gene flow between Spanish colonists and American Indians was established. Consequently, today more than 50 per cent of the population of Mexico, Honduras, Nicaragua, and Venezuela is hybrid and reflects this gene flow between Spaniard and Indian. We should also note that African Blacks form a significant portion of the stock from which hybrid populations in some parts of Central and South America, particularly Brazil, have arisen. In the United States, of course, beginning more than three hundred years ago, a European–African Black hybridization produced the American Black breeding population.

How hybrid a population is the American Black? Just what proportion of the gene pool in this population is European and how much is African? Blood-group analysis and population genetics have been used to arrive at some quantitative answers to these questions. Specifically, the method used was to measure the frequency with which a particular indicator gene appears in European, African Black, and American Black populations. The gene chosen was the Duffy factor. As seen in Table 6-4, this gene is virtually absent in the African Black populations from which slaves were taken for the New World. The frequency of Duffy in the European population is 43 per cent. The frequency of Duffy in a large group of American Blacks living in Oakland, California, was found to be 9.4 per cent. This gene could have come only from European sources be-

A: Duffy Frequencies in African Black, Caucasian, and American Black Populations

African Black Population of	Percentage of Duffy Positive
Upper Volta	0
Dahomey	0
Accra, Ghana	0
Lagos, Nigeria	0
Caucasians of West European ancestry	43

B: West European Duffy Frequency in American Blacks

	Percentage of Duffy Positive	Percentage of Caucasoid Contribution
American Blacks as a whole	9.2	21
Regional variations in American Black populations		
Charleston, South Carolina	3.7	4
Evans and Bullock Counties in Georgia	4.5	11
Oakland, California	9.4	22
Detroit, Michigan	11.1	26
New York, New York	8.1	19

Table 6-4.
Duffy Frequencies in Selected Populations

After T. E. Reed in *Science,* **165** (1969), p. 762.

cause it is absent in the stem populations of African Blacks in which the American Black finds parentage. Therefore, consideration of the frequency of this indicator gene allows us to assign Europe a contribution of approximately 20 per cent to the American Black gene pool and Africa a contribution of roughly 80 per cent. Other blood-group studies have ruled out the American Indian as a significant contributor to this gene pool.

The future course of this hybridization cannot be predicted. However, some biologists have speculated on the end results of complete hybridization between the present American Black population and the American White population. They have asked what Americans would look like if there were, say, thirty to forty generations during which race was not a factor in the selection of mating partners. The University of California geneticist Curt Stern has calculated the distribution of skin color in the American population after such a period of random mating (see Figure 6-6). In his calculation of color distribution, Stern assumed that skin color, like height and intelligence, is determined polygenically (that is to say, not by a single gene but by the interaction of many different genes). After such an amalgamation, the average color of the population would be only slightly darker than the average of today's American White population. The American Black would be gone from all but the history books of such a completely genetically integrated society.

What Color Will the Baby Be?

The calculations of Professor Stern make it quite clear that should the United States experience many generations of random mating between Blacks and Whites, the average skin color in the population will be only a shade darker than that displayed by its contemporary White population. Granting that this is the situation we would expect over a long period of time for the hybridization of the Black and White population, what might we expect in the short run when intermarriage between Blacks and Whites produce hybrid offspring?

This question was first examined in Jamaica by a team led by the American geneticist C. B. Davenport. They identified marriages in which one partner was White and the other Black and measured the skin color of these partners and of the racially hybrid offspring they produced. By such a study it was possible to examine the genetic determination of the capacity to produce melanin, a brown pigment that appears black when densely massed. Actually, everyone except albinos produces some melanin. The very fair produce

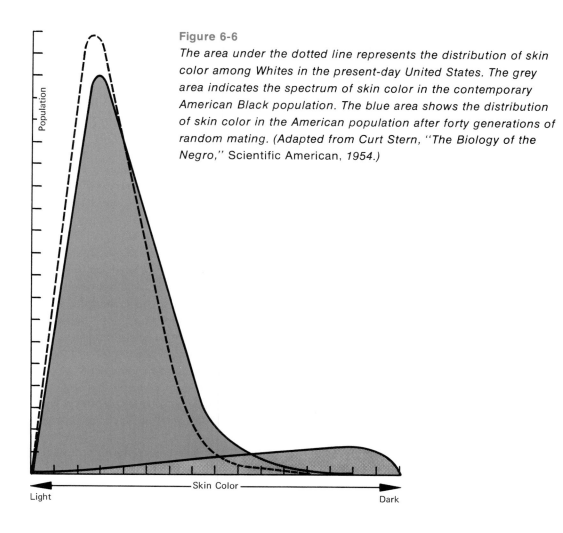

Figure 6-6

The area under the dotted line represents the distribution of skin color among Whites in the present-day United States. The grey area indicates the spectrum of skin color in the contemporary American Black population. The blue area shows the distribution of skin color in the American population after forty generations of random mating. (Adapted from Curt Stern, "The Biology of the Negro," Scientific American, 1954.)

Population

Skin Color

Light   Dark

very little and the Black produce a great deal. In conducting this study, Davenport and his colleagues deliberately selected interracial marriages in which the Black parent was a deep, rich ebony and the White parent alabaster fair. In interviews, none of the Black and White parents used in the study indicated any interracial ancestry. Davenport and his team found that the offspring of Black-White matings had skin colors intermediate between those of their parents. More recent studies conducted in England by Harrison and Owen, using a group of White Englishwomen and their West African Black husbands, have shown that the average pigmentation of the first-generation offspring was perhaps somewhat closer to that of the

White than to the Black parent. The emergence of three distinct classes, Black, White, and intermediate, is what one obtains when matings take place between White individuals with no Black ancestry and Black individuals with no White ancestry. For two reasons this is not the pattern one would expect to see in the offspring of many Black-White marriages here in the United States. The first of these reasons has to do with the fact that skin color is determined by not one but perhaps as many as five different pairs of genes. The second stems from the fact that the American Black population contains a significant (about 20 per cent as we saw earlier) fraction of Caucasoid genes. In the case of matings between pure-White and pure-Black individuals, the pure-Black individual donates five different genes that each specify highly pigmented skin, and the pure-White parent donates five different genes that each specify very light skin. The combination of a pure White and pure Black set results in an intermediate hue. The situation is much more complicated when one (or both) of the parents contains some genes specifying a dark skin color and some genes specifying a light skin color. The combination of such mixed gene sets give rise to offspring whose skin color can vary continuously between that of the darker and that of the lighter parent. Thus, it is possible for two individuals of dark complexion and mixed ancestry to produce children that are either of lighter or darker complexion than themselves. Offspring resulting from the mating of White individuals with no Black ancestry and Black individuals with some White ancestry will be of a hue intermediate between that of the Black and the White parent, with a strong likelihood that the child's skin color will be somewhat closer to that of the White than the dark-skinned parent.

We can conclude this discussion on skin color by noting that in discussing the inheritance in hybrid populations of skin color we haven't told the whole story. In most cases, a person's skin color is determined not solely by his genes but also, to some extent, by his environment. Everyone is familiar with the phenomenon of tanning on exposure to the sun. Many individuals genetically destined to be quite fair-skinned can make themselves brown as biscuits by a determined program of regular sunbathing. It is also true that Blacks who live in the northern, cloudy, low-sun environs of London are not so richly ebony-colored as they would be if they spent long days in the hot, bright Caribbean sun. What we see for skin color, of course, holds for many traits that have genetic determinants. There is often an interaction, sometimes quite strong, between hereditary and environmental factors to produce the phenotype that we actually see.

New hybrid populations are currently forming in several parts of the world. Notable examples are in Hawaii and Israel. In Hawaii today a hybridization of Mongoloid, Caucasoid, and Polynesian populations is in process. Given the relative geographical isolation of Hawaii, the development of a new hybrid breeding population may well continue.

In the new state of Israel many different populations of Jews, some of them isolated from each other since the time of the Diaspora, are again united. These different breeding populations have been drawn from Western and Eastern Europe, the Middle East, Africa, and Asia Minor. A glance at the data on blood-group frequencies and the distribution of a gene that causes a deficiency of a particular enzyme shows the multiracial composition of the Jewish

A: Blood Group Frequencies in Different Jewish Populations*

	Percentage of Type A	Percentage of Type B
Africa		
Morocco	22.7	16.4
Algeria	21.5	15.5
Libya	22.7	16.4
Europe		
Netherlands	25.9	6.2
Germany	27.1	11.5
Poland	28.5	12.5
Ukraine	28.7	12.4
Lithuania	25.5	13.0
Asia		
Yemen	17.4	9.5
Iran	25.9	18.5
Turkestan	20.8	21.6
Cochin (India)	11.6	14.3

Table 6-5.

Genetic Differences Among Jewish Populations

*From T. Dobzhansky, *Mankind Evolving* (New Haven, Conn.: Yale University Press, 1962).
†From a compilation by I. M. Lerner, *Heredity, Evolution and Society*. (San Francisco: Freeman, 1969).
**Glucose-6-phosphate dehydrogenase.

B: Frequency with Which a Gene Causing Deficiency of the Enzyme G6PD Appears in Various Jewish Populations in Israel†**

Kurdish	0.6
Persian and Iraqui	0.25
Turkish	0.05
Yemenite	0.05
European	0.02
North African	0.002

people (Table 6-5). Intermarriage and the consequent hybridization of these populations have already begun in Israel. Given the small geographical area and the isolation of a Jewish island in an Arab sea, the hybridization can be expected to continue. The end result will be an Israeli breeding population with its own characteristic gene frequencies.

The Health of Hybrids

Clearly, the hybridization of different human breeding populations is not a new idea; it is not exotic, untried, or an experiment whose outcome is unknown. Matings between races are facts of history. Solomon and Sheba provide the earliest and certainly the most distinguished recorded example. The colonization of the New World and the institution of slavery provided, as we have seen, a setting in which interracial hybridization took place on a massive scale. Today the mixed populations of Israel and Hawaii are proceeding briskly down the path of hybridization. In the New World and elsewhere, hybrid populations exist that number in the millions. These hybrid populations possess the reproductive competence and display the full range of human talents (and frailties) found in the parent populations.

The reasons for the health of hybrids of diverse parental types can be found in a consideration of man's adaptation to his environment. Today hybrid offspring between Caucasoid and Eskimo do not adapt to cold biologically but culturally, by turning up the thermostat. African Black–English Caucasoid hybrids living in London have no trouble getting enough vitamin D. It is available in milk and in vitamin pills. Racial differences such as those of skin color and body build, which were called into existence by forces of natural selection during the relatively culture-free period of man's development, do not confer survival value once cultural instead of biological solutions to these environmental challenges have been generally adopted.

Race Relations: A Family Tree

Earlier it was pointed out that differences in protein structure can be a kind of genetic litmus paper, extremely useful for estimating the genetic differences that exist between individuals or populations. During the last several years, careful analysis has shown that these differences also can be used to estimate the point in time when two different life forms diverged from a common ancestor. The more recently life forms have diverged, the smaller the number of differences their proteins show. Using such an approach, the work of such biochemical taxonomists as Doolittle, Blumenbach, and Mar-

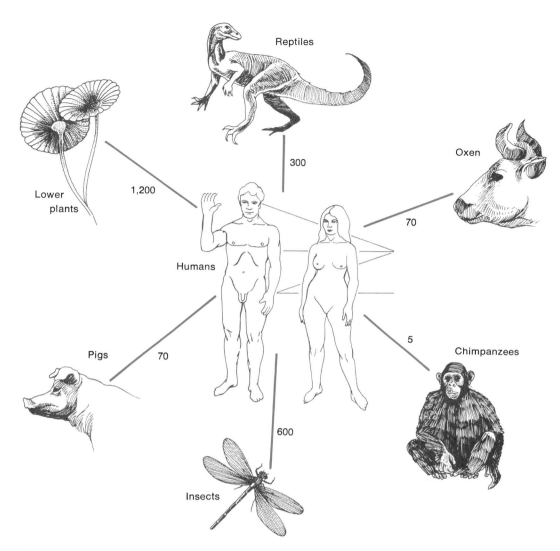

Figure 6-7

Separation of species in time. Biochemical differences in the structure of the same type of protein taken from contemporary representatives of the indicated type of organisms have allowed the time of divergence from a common ancestor to be estimated for each of these groups. The numbers give these separation intervals in millions of years.

goliash has told us much about the evolutionary distances that separate the diverse species found in today's world. This approach has produced the data used to construct Figure 6-7, which shows that humans have been separated in time from plants by more than

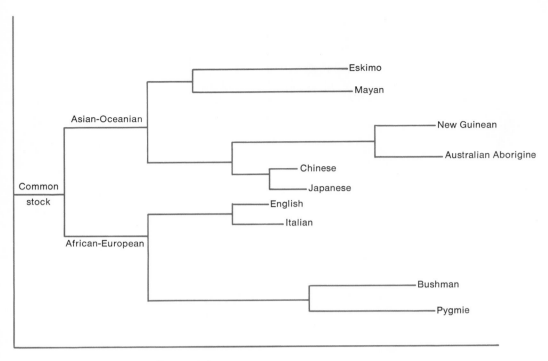

Figure 6-8
*Pedigree of ten populations. The relationships shown have been
determined by examination of the differences in structure evidenced
by samples of 58 different proteins that have been studied in these
populations. (Adapted from Cavalli-Sforza in* Scientific American,
September 1974.)

one billion years but that we only diverged from the same ancestral
stock as the chimpanzee some five or so million years ago.

Just as the molecular clock of differences in protein structure
can be applied to determine the separation in time of different species, Cavalli-Sforza and his colleagues have used it to locate in time
the approximate origin of some human racial stocks. As is shown
in Figure 6-8, they have examined the indicated populations for differences in the protein products of almost five dozen genes. Their
findings show that after divergence from a common human stock,
one branch gave rise to at least three distinct population groups: the
American Indian, the populations of China and Japan, and the aboriginal populations of Australia and New Guinea. The other branch
again forked to produce the populations of Europe and Africa.
Based on considerations of the rate at which proteins—the gene
products—accumulate differences, it can be estimated that the

racial stocks noted in Figure 6-8 have been separated from a common ancestor by no more than forty thousand years. Because modern man, *Homo sapiens,* emerged at least sixty thousand years ago and possibly more than one hundred thousand years ago, we can conclude that all the races of man emerged from a single human ancestor. Thus, biochemical genetics, while not finding that all men are brothers, certainly concludes that they are cousins and can be used to demonstrate that all the different races of man are merely twigs on the main branch of a common family tree.

7

race
and
mental
ability

Man has no biological capacity for flying and only a most unremarkable and rudimentary competence for either running or swimming. Yet, he excels at all three. He can fly higher longer, and farther than any bird. No fish can match the speed and certainty with which he navigates the seas. He routinely travels over the earth's surface at speeds in excess of a mile a minute for hours at a time. But, like the eagle, the marlin, and the prize-winning race horse, man too must thank natural selection for his conspicuous excellence. Instead of biological specializations for flying, swimming, or running, man has developed through evolution a highly specialized nervous system whose capstone is the human brain, a computer of unparalleled versatility and power. It can perceive problems and generate a desire to solve them. Through its accumulated experience and the power to recognize or even create relationships, it can solve problems. Furthermore, once having solved the problem, the brain can hold the organism on a course of action necessary to bring the solution to bear on the environment. Taken together, these mental abilities—drive, perception, intelligence, and will—reach a level in human populations not even approached by other animals. More than anything else, it is these mental abilities, uniquely and innately human, that isolate, elevate, and give dominion to mankind.

It would be difficult indeed to find a serious student of race or psychology who would not agree that the full range of these mental abilities is found in all the races of man. Differences of opinion may arise when one asks whether some races are "on the average" genetically more or less mentally able than other races. The analysis of this question must proceed in stages. First of all, it is necessary to determine whether and to what extent mental abilities are genetically determined. Because race is a genetic term, only the genetically inherited rather than the environmentally determined components of mental ability have any bearing on the question of inherent average racial differences. Therefore, any observed differences in racial populations that can be traced to cultural or environmental factors are without relevance to the question at hand.

It is apparent that to conduct an inquiry into the inheritance of a trait we must have some means of observing and measuring it. For measurements of traits such as blood type or fingerprint pattern, the measuring techniques are precise, objective, and do not require the active participation of the subject under examination. Furthermore, marked differences in the environmental histories of the subjects do not affect their blood type or change their basic fingerprint patterns. Tools for the measurement of mental abilities like intelligence or of factors such as drive or will that bear on personality are much less satisfactory. Although personality tests exist that include components of what we loosely called drive and will, they are not precisely quantitative and are quite sensitive to environmental influences. The IQ test, which measures components of what we call intelligence, is the most widely used of psychological tests and the best established test of a particular mental ability. Unfortunately, as we shall see, its results too can be significantly affected by environment. We know that the scores made on intelligence tests are sensitive to the nature of the home and school environment in which intellectual development takes place. The effect on IQ test performance of other environmental factors such as poor nutrition in the pre- and postnatal phases of child development and cross-cultural differences between racial, ethnic, and income groups are areas of active investigation from which more information can be expected.

Realizing that our tools are fewer than needed and are imperfectly controlled, let us begin our inquiry into what is known about race and mental ability. We shall focus our discussion on the components of that particular mental ability, intelligence, that are measured by IQ tests. We center on intelligence solely because out of the complex of recognized mental abilities, it is the one for which the most information, especially of a comparative nature, is available.

We should realize at the outset that even though IQ scores are useful in predicting trainability for various occupations, they are not very useful for predicting success. Once the training or educational process is completed, factors other than intelligence operate to determine success. The leaders in a field, whether it be banking or biology, are not necessarily those with the highest IQs. Given a sufficiently high IQ to complete the training in a particular field with high competence, other factors such as character and personality become the determinants in the attainment of highest eminence.

The Nature of Intelligence

[Intelligence is] the ability to combine and separate.
— St. Thomas Aquinas

[Intelligence is the ability] to see the difference between things which are similar and to see the similarities between things which seem different.
— Arthur R. Jensen

The ability to synthesize apparently discordant or unrelated experiences and observations and to decompose the apparently unitary into its constituent parts is not itself a single entity. It can be separated into a number of constituent abilities. One of these is memory, the ability to store and recall information of various sorts. Another is the ability to perform logical operations on stored or incoming information. Still another is the ability to divine and conceptualize spatial relationships. Indeed, some students of intelligence see the capacity to synthesize and decompose as a three-dimensional matrix containing many constituent and interacting abilities. The intelligence test is a performance test in which some of these abilities are sampled.

Intelligence testing was begun in 1905 when Alfred Binet, a distinguished French psychologist, and Theodore Simon, a physician, were commissioned by the French government to design a test to determine a child's likelihood of success in school. These pioneering workers designed a test that required those taking it to tackle a variety of problems involving memory, verbal facility, reasoning, and language comprehension. The Binet-Simon procedure, and Binet's later modifications of it, satisfactorily accomplished the purposes for which it was designed: the identification of the slow learners in Paris schools. The success of the procedure attracted the attention of colleagues in other lands and within a few years Professor Binet's "intelligence test" was exported to other countries, including the United States, where it underwent a continuing process of modification and refinement. Initially intended as a tool for predicting school performance in the French school system, within a few years of its introduction in the United States, its application was broadened to include, after 1914, the evaluation of the mental abilities of inductees into the armed forces. Beginning with its use for the mass evaluation of armed forces personnel during the World War I, intelligence testing underwent a transformation from a limited and modest procedure into a highly sophisticated educational tool of technology. It was here in the United States that Terman and his colleagues at Stanford first formulated a quantitative shorthand for rating performance on an intelligence test, the IQ. As indicated here, originally intelligence tests were designed to be given to children, and the score received was dubbed by Terman the intelligence quotient, or IQ. In the early years, it was defined as the ratio of the child's mental age to his chronological age, multiplied by 100 ($IQ = MA/CA \times 100$). It provided a quantitative measure of the contrast between the child's mental growth and his chronological age. For instance, if one examined a four-year-old boy and found he could do all the tasks performed by the average six-year-old, he would have an IQ of 150 ($^6/_4 \times 100 = 150$). Because the development of intrinsic mental powers, very much like the attainment of adult height, is essentially completed by the late teens, mental ages above 16 have little or no meaning. Thus, when a fifty-year-old receives a score of 150 on an IQ test, it does not mean he has a mental age of 75. Rather, it means that, in the distribution of performances on intelligence tests, he falls at a position on the normal curve that is far above the average and corresponds to an IQ of 150.

Most students of intelligence feel that it is the aggregate expression of the interaction of an enormous variety of components. Indeed, one of the leading students of intelligence, J. P. Guilford, represents intelligence as an interacting matrix of 120 factors (see Figure 7-1). In his model, intelligence is the interaction of certain operations with what he calls products that have a content that may be figural, symbolic, semantic, or behavioral. For instance, the recollection of the Pythagorean theorem would be intelligent behavior involving the operation of memory, the product labeled relations in the diagram, and the content that is symbolic. Obviously, many types of behavior we would describe as intelligent involve other, far more complicated, interactions between these basic types of elements shown in the model. The IQ test is designed to sample a number, although certainly not all, of these types of interactions. It is deliberately constructed so that most of the IQ scores fall close to a median value of 100. This value is called the average intelligence and, under ideal conditions, a population taking the test will have the normal, or bell-shaped, distribution shown in Figure 7-2. Indeed, we can expect that in any population with a mean score of 100, 50 per cent of that population will have scores

Figure 7-1

The structure of intellect. (Modified from J. P. Guilford, The Nature of Intelligence. *New York: McGraw-Hill, 1967.)*

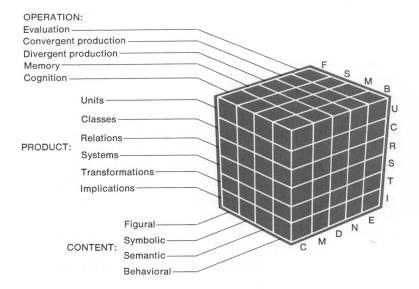

OPERATION:
Evaluation
Convergent production
Divergent production
Memory
Cognition

PRODUCT:
Units
Classes
Relations
Systems
Transformations
Implications

CONTENT:
Figural
Symbolic
Semantic
Behavioral

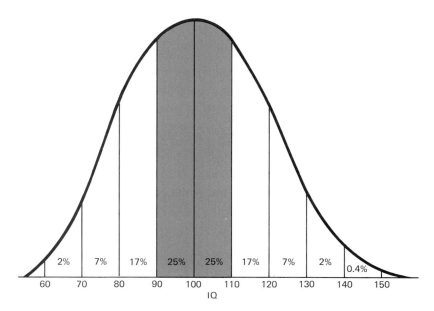

| 2% | 7% | 17% | 25% | 25% | 17% | 7% | 2% | 0.4% |
| 60 | 70 | 80 | 90 | 100 | 110 | 120 | 130 | 140 | 150 |

IQ

Figure 7-2

The normal distribution of IQ scores. Fifty per cent of the population lies in the range of 90 to 110. Very few receive scores above 150 or below 60.

between 90 and 110. These individuals are said to have scores in the normal, or average, range. One quarter of the population will be expected to score above this average range and the remaining quarter will have IQs below it. IQ tests are constructed by assembling a collection of tasks of varying difficulty, each of which is largely independent of the others. Difficulty is determined by administering the items to a number of individuals in a reference population. Those items that almost everyone, say eight out of ten, answers correctly are considered easy. On the other hand, a question that is only answered correctly by one in twenty is considered quite difficult. Those items that are so easy that everyone answers them correctly, or are so difficult that no one answers them correctly, are not useful for distributing people according to ability, and so are not included on the test. Once a suitable assortment of test items has been assembled into an IQ test, the normal, or average, range of IQ scores is determined by administering this test to a reference population. The raw scores (the number of items they actually get right) received by this reference population are used to establish a distribution similar to that in Figure 7-2. The raw score corresponding to the median of the distribution is assigned an IQ of 100. All other raw scores above and below 100 are assigned IQ scores appropriate to their position in the distribution. This allows one to establish a scale for the conversion of raw scores made on the test into IQs. The IQ scores of all persons taking the test are then computed by using the scale established in the reference population. This scale is used even though these individuals are outside the reference population and may differ in many respects from it.

The use of reference populations to set scales and performance standards for IQ tests introduces some difficulties in interpreting scores from groups that differ markedly from the reference population. In the United States, reference populations are composed primarily of representatives who are White and middle class or lower middle class. We have obvious problems that stem from the differences in home and social environment when we apply these tests to such populations as Puerto Ricans, Mexican Americans, American Indians, and American Blacks. This is also true when we apply the test to Whites from backgrounds of profound disadvantage or extreme cultural and intellectual poverty such as that found in some rural environments. Clearly, differences in the experience of certain testees might make the application of a standard scale, established in a particular kind of reference population, an unrealistic way of evaluating their intrinsic ability.

Those involved in IQ testing recognize that cultural differences do exist between different groups in a population as diverse economically, geographically, and racially as that found in the United States. These differences mean that many experiences common to some will be unfamiliar or even unknown to others. An upper-middle-class, Eastern-born, ivy-league-educated stockbroker who has grown up in an environment that has enabled him to develop an ear for baroque music, a taste for the wines of the Bordeaux, and an eye for Dubuffet, might reasonably be expected to have been exposed to, and at home with, the information and practices of his class. A rather different store of information would be accumulated by a Black numbers runner on the South Side of Chicago, who, in the course of surviving, has accumulated a knowledge of which policemen can be bought and which ones can't, how to avoid being robbed when carrying the day's proceeds, and where to get really good barbeque. There can be little argument with the proposition that an intelligence test that relies heavily on either the store of information accumulated by the stockbroker or the numbers runner will not fairly test the aptitude of the other. There is now abroad in intelligence testing the notion of culture-loaded and culture-free tests. In the culture-loaded tests there are items that depend on the information, vocabulary, and experiences of a particular culture. In the culture-free IQ tests, the items are nonverbal and usually require discernment of geometrical relationships or patterns. In the survey of IQ test approaches presented shortly, three of the approaches—the *Dove Counterbalance Test of General Intelligence,* parts of the *Wechsler Adult Intelligence Scale,* and parts of the *California Test of Mental Maturity*—have significant amounts of culture loading. The other approach, that used by *Raven's Progressive Matrices,* is a test in which the content is relatively lacking in culture loading. However, it should be borne in mind that there is one essential ingredient, motivation, that cannot be removed from the test situation.

Determining a person's IQ is not like determining his blood type. Blood types can be determined with or without the active cooperation or involvement of the individual. One need only obtain a sample of blood, forcibly, if necessary, and submit it to the well-defined and highly standardized procedure that gives an absolute determination of A, B, or O blood type. Determining a person's IQ, on the other hand, is very much like determining how fast the individual can run. If we ask an individual to cover a race course of 100 yards and he does so in 10 seconds or less, we can conclude that the individual is very fast indeed. But, on the other hand, if it takes him 20 seconds, or perhaps 100 seconds, the individual may be slow, ill, or merely uncooperative. The same thing is true with an IQ test. If an individual scores far above the average on an IQ test, say 150 or 160, we can conclude that that individual has considerable abilities in the areas examined by the test and could further predict his probable success in many academic programs. However, when an individual does not score so highly, it may reflect inability to do so or failure to do so for reasons other than lack of ability. One of these reasons could be conscious or (to borrow a term from psychoanalytic practice) unconscious lack of motivation. It is, of course, possible that some cultures place a higher value on, and take more seriously, exercises such as IQ tests than do others. If such differences in motivation do exist, then the one component of culture loading that contributes importantly to differences in performance has nothing to do with the content of the test. That is to say, it doesn't matter whether one is asking about the cooking of chitlins or the symphonies of Beethoven; it doesn't matter whether one is manipulating syllogisms or trying to determine which figure comes next, a star or a square. What is important is the perception of the test situation itself and the subject's reaction to it. Unfortunately, we do not, in fact could not, quantitatively measure the motivational load of individuals taking IQ tests. Until we can do so, it will not be possible to exclude from consideration the possibility that individuals from different cultural backgrounds respond differently to IQ tests or parts of IQ tests due to differences in factors such as motivation.

IQ tests are performance tests that seek to determine an individual's capacity to grasp and manipulate a number of different types of concepts. They are of two types: individual and group. The individual tests are designed to be administered to a single individual during a private conference with a trained examiner. Group IQ tests may be simultaneously administered to any number of individuals ranging from one or two up to several hundred or even several thousand. Although the reliability of individually administered tests is superior to that of group tests, considerations of time and economy of manpower make it necessary on occasion to employ a group test of intelligence.

Here we examine the approaches to the measurement of IQ taken by three tests generally used and one that does not find general application.

1. The *Wechsler Adult Intelligence Scale* (WAIS) is a test that is individually administered. It samples a number of verbal and nonverbal abilities. As one will see from the samples, some of the tasks the testee is required to perform have a component of content culture loading that can be quite strong.
2. The *California Test of Mental Maturity* is a group IQ test that samples a broad range of abilities. Some of the items included are seen to have strong content culture loading also.
3. *Raven's Progressive Matrices* is a group test that depends primarily on one's ability to comprehend relationships. It is totally nonverbal and has little content culture loading.
4. The *Dove Counterbalance Test of General Intelligence* is a somewhat tongue-in-cheek parody of IQ testing in which the vocabulary and situations used in the exercises are drawn from the Black street culture.

Wechsler Adult Intelligence Scale (WAIS)

This test consists of eleven subtests:

Part I. Verbal Tests
  a. Information
  b. Comprehension
  c. Arithmetic
  d. Similarities
  e. Digit Span
  f. Vocabulary

Part II. Performance Tests
  g. Digit Symbol
  h. Picture Completion
  i. Block Design
  j. Picture Arrangement
  k. Object Assembly

Examples similar to those included in the verbal tests of the WAIS appear here.[1] Note that some of the items, including many of those under Information and Vocabulary, are strongly culture loaded. However, the items under Digit Span have considerably less culture loading, as do many of the tasks one is asked to perform in Part II, the performance portion of the test. Because the performance tests require special equipment, they do not appear here.

Sample questions from the WAIS verbal tests:
a. Information
    1. Name three men who have been Presidents of the United States since the Second World War.
    2. How many years are there in a century?
    3. How far is it from New York to San Francisco?
    4. Who wrote *The Decline and Fall of the Roman Empire?*
    5. What is the Bhagavad-Gita?
b. Comprehension
    1. Why do most people avoid carrying large sums of cash?
    2. Why does the state require people to license automobiles?
    3. What does this saying mean? "Bashful beggars have empty pockets."
c. Arithmetic
    1. If a person bought three newspapers at 15¢ each, how much was spent?
       (Solve in 15 seconds)
    2. How many feet are there in 100 yards?
       (Solve in 30 seconds)
    3. A person sold a car for three fifths of what it cost new. If $2,400 was received, how much did the car cost new?
       (Solve in one minute)
d. Similarities
    1. In what way are a house and a tent alike?
    2. In what way are a symphony and a painting alike?
    3. In what way is a snowflake like an ice cube?
e. Digit Span
    1. Digits Forward
        (a) On hearing 3 digits (i.e., 4–7–5) recall and repeat them.
        (b) On hearing 6 digits (i.e., 5–6–2–7–8–9) recall and repeat them.
        (c) On hearing 9 digits (i.e., 3–7–3–4–3–8–9–2–1) recall and repeat them.
    2. Digits Backward
        (a) On hearing 2 digits (i.e., 5–8) recall and repeat them backward.
        (b) On hearing 4 digits (i.e., 2–1–7–9) recall and repeat them backward.

[1]Adapted from David Wechsler, *Wechsler Adult Intelligence Scale* (New York: The Psychological Corporation, 1955).

(c) On hearing 8 digits (i.e., 3–1–5–6–9–4–3–5) recall and repeat them backward.

   f. Vocabulary

      1. What does lunch mean?   4. What does insidious mean?

      2. What does devour mean?   5. What does etiology mean?

      3. What does peerless mean?

California Test of Mental Maturity[2]

1. Opposites

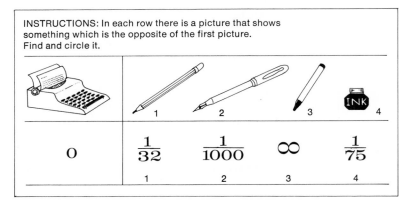

2. Similarities

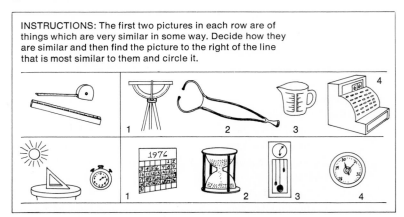

[2]Adapted from the 1963 Revision Level 5 of the *California Test of Mental Maturity* devised by Elizabeth T. Sullivan, Willis W. Clark, and Ernest W. Teagues. Published by the California Test Bureau, a division of McGraw-Hill.

3. Number Series

INSTRUCTIONS: The numbers in each row increase or decrease according to a rule. However, in each row there is an extra number that does not belong. Find the number that should be omitted among the answer numbers and circle it.

| 7 | 10 | 13 | 19 | 25 | 31 | | 10 | 13 | 25 | 31 |
| 1/3 | 1/6 | 1/9 | 1/81 | 1/6561 | | | 1/3 | 1/6 | 1/81 | 1/6561 |

4. Number Problems

INSTRUCTIONS: Solve these problems. You may use scratch paper if necessary. Circle the correct answer.

1. George worked 3 days and made a total of $57. If he made $15 on the first day and $21 on the second day, how much did he make on the third day?   (a) $16   (b) $25   (c) $21   (d) $10

2. A farmer wishes to farm in his cow pasture which is a rectangle 300 feet long and 100 feet wide. If fencing material sells for $1.50 a yard, how much will it cost the farmer to fence in his pasture?   (a) $1500   (b) $200   (c) $400   (d) $800

5. Vocabulary

INSTRUCTIONS: Circle the word that does not mean the same or about the same as the first word.

1. enjoin	(a) order	2. paramount	(a) dominant
	(b) command		(b) predominant
	(c) link		(c) preponderant
	(d) direct		(d) preposses
3. interpose	(a) insinuate	4. dementia	(a) mania
	(b) introduce		(b) insanity
	(c) intercalate		(c) demeanor
	(d) intractable		(d) psychoses

Raven's Progressive Matrices[3]

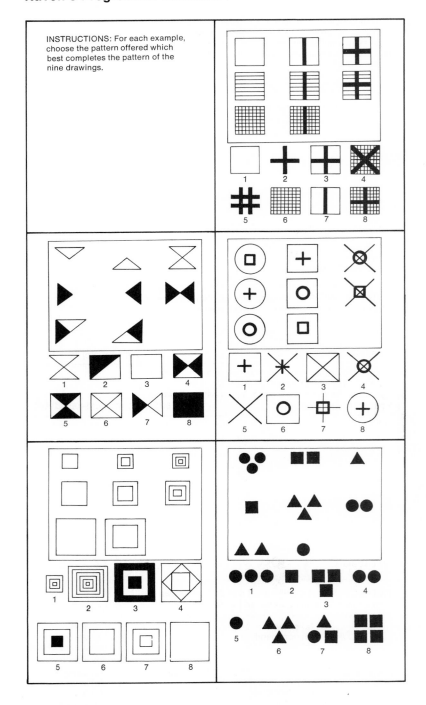

INSTRUCTIONS: For each example, choose the pattern offered which best completes the pattern of the nine drawings.

[3]After John C. Raven, *Advanced Progressive Matrices Set II* (London: H. K. Lewis and Co., Ltd. 1962). Used with permission of the Executors of the Estate of Dr. J. C. Raven.

Dove Counterbalance Test of General Intelligence[4]

1. If a man is called a "Blood," then he is a _____.
   (a) Fighter
   (b) Mexican-American
   (c) Black
   (d) Hungry Hemophile
   (e) Redman or Indian

2. Cheap chitlins (not the kind you purchase at a frozen-food counter) will taste rubbery unless they are cooked long enough. How soon can you quit cooking them to eat and enjoy them?
   (a) 45 minutes
   (b) 2 hours
   (c) 24 hours
   (d) 1 week (on a low flame)
   (e) 1 hour

3. "Bird" or "Yardbird" was the "jacket" that jazz lovers from coast to coast hung on _____.
   (a) Lester Young
   (b) Peggy Lee
   (c) Benny Goodman
   (d) Charlie Parker
   (e) "Birdman of Alcatraz"

4. Hattie Mae Johnson is on the County. She has four children and her husband is now in jail for non-support as he was unemployed and was not able to give her money. Her welfare check is now $286.00 per month. Last night she went out with the biggest player in town. If she got pregnant, then nine months from now, how much more will her welfare check be?
   (a) $80.00
   (b) $2.00
   (c) $35.00
   (d) $150.00
   (e) $100.00

5. Did the "Beatles" have soul?
   (a) Yes
   (b) No
   (c) Gee whiz or maybe

6. A "handkerchief head" is _____.
   (a) A cool cat
   (b) A porter
   (c) An Uncle Tom
   (d) A hoddi
   (e) A preacher

7. "Jet" is _____.
   (a) An "East Oakland' motorcycle club
   (b) One of the gangs in West Side Story

[4]A measure of the cultural involvement of poor folks and Black street cultures.

(c) A news and gospel magazine

(d) A way of life for the very rich

Fill in the missing word or words that sound best:

8. "Tell it like it _____."
   (a) Thinks I am
   (b) Baby
   (c) Try
   (d) Is
   (e) Y'all
9. "Bo-Diddley' is a _____.
   (a) game for children
   (b) down home cheap wine
   (c) down home singer
   (d) new dance
   (e) Meojoe call
10. Which word is the most out of place here?
    (a) Brother
    (b) Blood
    (c) Grey
    (d) Spook
    (e) Black
11. True or False: A pimp is also a young man who lays around all day.
    (a) Yes
    (b) No

The Inheritance of IQ

Memory, symbol manipulation, and logical processes are all functions of that part of the nervous system known as the brain. The basic specifications for the brain and other parts of the nervous system are laid down in the genes, as they are for the rest of the body. It would not be surprising, therefore, if expressions of its function, such as mental ability, also showed strong patterns of inheritance. Indications that mental abilities may have strong heritable components are provided by a number of isolated examples of patterns of excellence in particular families. In this regard, the noted biologist and humanist philosopher Theodosius Dobzhansky cites the Bach family as an illustration. Of the fifty-four male ancestors, relatives, and descendants of the great composer and virtuoso Johann Sebastian Bach, forty-six were professional musicians. Seventeen of these were composers, some—Karl Philipp Emanuel and Johann Christian come immediately to mind—enjoyed distinction. Although there can be little doubt that birth into a musical family helped to direct the male Bachs into the making of music, the almost uniform success they experienced also suggests the possession of enabling constitutional factors.

Other families such as the Darwins or the Huxleys of England could also be cited. But these examples, although numerous, would not by themselves be thoroughly convincing. Sons, after all inherit more than genes from their fathers. In addition to the chromosomes, there is often a cultural and economic heritage. In this connection, we note that bank presidencies, like musical accomplishments, also run in families. But few would argue that the inheritance of business acumen and fiscal wizardry are the determining factors in the meteoric rise of the president's son from the teller's cage to the executive suite. Most reasonable observers would conclude that the inheritance of a name, not a collection of DNA molecules, was the crucial factor.

Studies of identical twins provide the most powerful tools for the investigation of the inheritance of traits. Although not so interesting as poking around in the family trees of the eminent, such studies have a much greater potential for yielding data whose interpretation and significance can be tested by rigorous scientific analysis. The rationale for the use of identical twins in the investigation of the inheritance of intelligence is outlined here.

Twins are of two sorts, identical and fraternal. Identical twins come from a single egg, fertilized by a single sperm. The single zygote formed from the union divides to produce a group of genetically identical cells. In the course of further growth and development, this colony of cells gives rise to two genetically identical embryos. Thus, identical twins have identical stores of genetic information. Fraternal twins develop when two different eggs are each fertilized by two different sperms. Fraternal twins, even though communally gestated and simultaneously born, are no more closely related to each other than to other children in the family. By including observations made on twins who have suffered the personal tragedy of being separated soon after birth and adopted into different homes, one assumes that although endowed with identical genetic complements, members of the twin pair will experience significantly different environments. We can determine the degree to which measurements of the same character are associated in each twin of a pair by using correlation coefficients. A correlation coefficient is a mathematical way of expressing the degree of association or coupling between two observations. For example, there is close coupling between rain and overcast skies. If it rained every time the sky were overcast, the correlation coefficient would be 1.0. However, this is not the case. Although there is a higher probability of rain when skies are overcast than when they are sunny, precipitation is not certain on cloudy days. Consequently, the correlation coefficient that gives a quantitative estimate of the coupling between cloud cover and rain is high, but less than 1.0. Generally speaking, a correlation coefficient of 0.70 or higher indicates close coupling, whereas a coefficient of less than 0.30 indicates that the coupling is weak. Provided certain critical assumptions hold true, we can, by appropriate mathematical manipulation of the correlation coefficient for a particular trait in pairs of identical twins, obtain a quantitative estimate of the degree to which that trait is controlled by heredity. This index of inheritance is called the heritability.

The heritability tells us what proportion of the variation we see in a trait is determined by variation in the genes of the population in which we are studying the trait. It can assume a range of values from 0, where there is no genetic contribution, up to 1.0, when the environment makes no contribution. The variation in blood type we see in a population can be accounted for entirely by genetic differences among members of the population. Blood type is, therefore, under total genetic control and has a heritability of 1.0. On the other hand, the assignment of Social Security numbers to members of a population is under total environmental control. It has no genetic component whatever and, consequently, has a heritability of 0.0.

A compilation of the heritabilities in White populations of a number of traits is shown in Table 7-1. Because, as we will see subsequently, heritabilities may differ between different races of the same species, it is important to bear in mind that the data presented in Table 7-1 applies to White populations only. One may surmise that heritabilities for particular traits such as height will be similarly high in other races, but it should be borne in mind that such extensions

Table 7-1.
Inheritance in Twins

Modified and adapted with additions from T. Dobzhansky, *Mankind Evolving* (New Haven, Conn.: Yale University Press, 1962), p. 85.

Trait	Correlation Coefficients			
	Fraternal Twins	Identical Twins Reared Together	Identical Twins Reared Apart	Heritability (Simple)
Blood type		1.0	1.0	1.0
Sitting height	0.50	0.96	0.88	0.77
Standing height	0.64	0.97	0.93	0.86
Weight	0.63	0.92	0.87	0.76
IQ	0.62	0.92	0.73	0.53
Word meaning	0.56	0.86		
Arithmetic computation	0.69	0.73		
Nature study and science	0.65	0.77		
Spelling	0.73	0.87		

are surmise and hypothetical until data, appropriately collected and correctly interpreted, demonstrate that the extension is indeed valid. Examination of the data in Table 7-1 suggests that genes are responsible for a significant (but not total) portion of the variation in IQ seen in White populations.

It is on the issue of the heritability of IQ that the race-IQ argument turns. Therefore, it is important to be aware of some of the chameleonlike properties of heritability and to appreciate some of the methodological pitfalls that have entrapped those who have sought accurately to determine the heritability of IQ.

It is important to realize that the heritability of a trait is not necessarily fixed for each trait displayed by a species. The value of the heritability of some traits may differ from race to race. Within the same race of a species the heritability of some traits may change as the environment in which development takes place is changed. Let us examine the thoughts of two individuals, both eminent, who hold different views on the issue of race and intelligence. The following quotations by Curt Stern and by Arthur Jensen show that they at least agree on the mutability of heritability.

And it deserves repeating that heritability is not a fixed attribute of a trait but may vary widely in different populations and with time in the same population.[5]

Heritability . . . is not a constant like π and the speed of light. . . . Estimates of H (heritability) are specific to the population sampled, the point in time, how the measurements were made, and the particular test used to obtain the measurements.[6]

To demonstrate the reality of these caveats, with regard to the constancy of heritability, consider the following example. Coat color in the Siamese cat is determined by genes, just as in other varieties of cats. However, the extent to which these genes are expressed in this particular race of cats is strongly modified by the environmental variable, temperature. Exposure to cold causes the coat, particularly along the tips of the extremities, to darken. Let us suppose that an investigator wanted to determine the inheritance of coat color in the Siamese cat. Let us suppose further that the investigator was unaware of the role played by temperature in modifying the expression of genes for coat color and so studied the inheritance of coat color in genetically identical Siamese cats who were not all exposed to

[5]Curt Stern, *Human Genetics*, 3rd ed. (San Francisco: Freeman, 1974).
[6]Arthur Jensen in *The Harvard Educational Review*, 1969.

the same temperature. His data would lead him to calculate a value for the heritability of coat color that would be lower than the value obtained by another investigator who maintained the animals in the same thermal environment. The fact that the expression of coat color is temperature-sensitive makes it easy to appreciate that the phenotype we see is often an expression of the interaction of genetic and environmental factors. Furthermore, this particular feature—the interaction of the temperature sensitivity of the coat color genes and environment—is seen in a particular race of cat, the Siamese, but not in other races such as the Manx, the Angora, or the Persian. It is clear from this simple illustration that heritabilities, even for simple characteristics such as coat color, measured in one race should not cavalierly be assumed to apply to other races of the same species. A moment's reflection leads one to the conclusion that it would not be at all surprising to find that the heritability of so complex a set of traits as those that contribute to what we call IQ, interacting with so complex and variable a set of environments as those inhabited by humankind, could vary in the same population and differ between populations.

In addition to the potential for variation inherent in heritability, we will see that the determination of the value of heritability from identical twin studies is plagued by an inherent methodological uncertainty. Earlier we indicated that identical twins separated soon after birth and raised in different environments have been a favorite tool of investigators interested in measuring the heritability of traits such as IQ. At the core of this methodology employing separated identical twins are two assumptions. (1) both twins have identical genes and (2) the environments in which they are separately reared are no more similar than those of unrelated individuals. It is argued by these investigators that studies with identical twins provide a system in which environment is the only variable because both twins have identical hereditary endowments. It is assumed that, once separated, identical twins experience environments no more similar than those of unrelated strangers. There is no reason to question the assumption that identical twins have identical genes. What can be questioned is the assumption that the environments experienced by separated pairs of identical twins are no more similar than those of unrelated persons. This assumption of uncorrelated environments does not hold for two reasons: (1) a consequence of adoption patterns and (2) the fact that identical twins are constitutionally so similar.

With respect to adoption patterns, examination of the degree of "separation" experienced by identical twins adopted into different homes is usually not nearly so great as would be the case if they were randomly handed out on street corners. In his book, *The Science and Politics of IQ,* the distinguished psychologist Leon J. Kamin has examined some of the "classic" studies of IQ in "separately" reared identical twins. In his examination of a study by J. Shields[7] of forty pairs of identical twins who were separated soon after birth, Kamin found that for the majority of the cases reported the degree of separation was far less than ideal. In twenty-seven out of the forty cases examined, the twins were brought up in related branches of the parents' families. In some cases, the circumstances of the separated twins were as follows:

A. Benjamin and Ronald were separated at nine months. They were both brought up in the same village, one brother by the parents and the other by the grandmother.

B. Jesse and Winifred were separated at three months and brought up within a few hundred yards of each other.

C. Bertram and Christopher were separated at birth and brought up by two of the father's sisters, each of whom reared one of the twins in her home. The sisters lived next door to each other in a small English village.

These examples, although extreme, are culled from the pages of one of the "landmark" studies often cited as demonstrating the high heritability of IQ. It illustrates a difficulty in many studies of IQ heritability that involve adoption. The adoption process is not usually a random one in which children are dispersed to the four corners of the globe without regard to the temperament or situation of the adopting family. Adoption agencies rightfully seek to place children in stable homes where they will be loved and properly cared for. This tends to be a factor that decreases the variation in the environments into which children are likely to be adopted. Because the beauty of studies on identical twins separated at birth rests heavily on the assumption that they are reared in uncorrelated environments, the tendency of adoption practices to introduce correlations is a serious one that must always be considered in interpreting such studies.

Problems of the nonrandomness of adoption aside, a bit of reflection will indicate how difficult it is for two human beings as similar as identical twins to avoid some environmental similarities even if from birth they had been reared at opposite ends of the country and never saw each other. The almost complete correlation of physiology and physiognomy between identical twins causes them to perceive and interact with their environment in many ways that are similar. This somewhat crude example may illustrate the point.

---

[7]J. Shields, *Monozygotic Twins Brought Up Apart and Brought Up Together* (London: Oxford University Press, 1962).

Suppose a set of identical twins is separated at birth and reared separately, one in Boston and the other in Chicago. They never see each other, or for that matter don't know they are members of an identical twin pair. Suppose they are each in the neighborhood of seven feet tall. Can we assume that because they were separated at birth and reared apart their environments were uncorrelated, or at least no more correlated than that of two strangers who happen to be riding on the same subway or flying in the same airplane? Clearly we cannot. Both will live, or try to live, in surroundings especially tailored for the very tall. It is likely that people who coach basketball teams will have tried to interest them in the sport. They will have spent most of their lives ducking doorjambs; folding into Volkswagens; being looked up to by, and looking down on, their fellowmen; and purchasing clothing that is always too short. Without citing further examples that could, of course, be multiplied, would any reasonable individual conclude that these persons don't live in correlated environments?

It is true that most identical twin pairs do not share so dramatic a trait as seven-foot stature. Nevertheless, one is led, inescapably, to the conclusion that because of their extraordinary similarity they will interact with and be acted on by their environments in ways that are similar. This will be generally true whether they are raised together or reared apart. In short, identical twins separated at birth do not necessarily experience uncorrelated environments. The assumption at the heart of studies of correlations between the IQs of identical twins separated at birth is that, although genetically identical, they are reared in environments no more correlated than those of unrelated persons. Earlier we learned that, in practice, this is rarely the case. Now we find that, even if it were uniformly the case, the environments experienced by identical twins are likely to be more correlated than those of unrelated persons. This methodological complication inherent in identical-twin studies colors with ambiguity heritability measurements employing identical twins.

At this point we may be driven to ask, are the genes to any extent responsible for the differences in IQ we see between different individuals? Put another way, we might ask, is IQ to any extent heritable? It is difficult to believe that a behavior — performance on an IQ test — that relies so heavily on the functioning of the central nervous system (and particularly that part of the central nervous system we call the brain, whose basic architecture and composition is genetically determined) would not depend to some extent on genes? And just as some individuals receive superior genetic endowments for throwing a football or a punch, it seems reasonable to suppose that some might inherit a nervous system better suited to determining relations between words and figures or manipulating ideas and symbols than others. On the other hand, no one would argue that athletes with the innate potential for their sport of a Kareem Abdul Jabbar or a Bill Walton would have developed into the superb basketball players they are without the nurturing environment of UCLA's "college of basketball knowledge" and the teaching of its famed coach "Professor" John Wooten. Similarly, one would suppose that intelligence as measured by IQ tests depends on the nurturing environment and that, unquestionably, some of the differences we note in the IQs of different individuals reflect differences in the totality of their experiences.

So far little of what is claimed here would cause truly deep controversy. Difficulties will arise when one tries to say with certainty that a given percentage of the difference between the IQs of different individuals is due to differences in their genetic endowments. The methodological difficulties, two of which we have discussed at some length, are formidable and, at this time, deny the field of behavioral genetics the certain and precise knowledge of the heritability of IQ. It is a matter about which experts deeply engaged in the field of behavioral genetics fail to agree. Furthermore, simply making more measurements or collecting more data won't resolve the disputes, which are, at this writing, so common in this area. There are those who feel that the existing techniques for determining the heritability of IQ are inadequate to establish precise results. Now, with some appreciation for the problems that surround the precise assessment of the contribution of genetic endowment to the variation in IQs of individuals, we turn to a consideration of the role, if any, played by heredity in accounting for the mean IQ differences among races.

Race and IQ

Many of the races of man are represented in large numbers in the population of the United States. In addition to Whites, Blacks, and Orientals, there are American Indians and such fairly distinct ethnic groups as Mexican Americans and Puerto Ricans. Because the mass administration of IQ tests has been practiced in this country for a number of years, it is possible to compare the performances of these groups with each other. When such a comparison is made, we find that the highest average scores are compiled by White and Oriental populations and the lowest average scores by the other American minorities. These are over-all differences computed for the total populations tested in each group. When we compare subgroups of these various populations with each other, we find different distributions. For instance, even though the average IQ recorded by the total White population exceeds that of the American Black population, Black populations in certain northeastern locations achieve higher average scores than Whites in some areas of the rural South. But, when we consider the over-all distributions, it is clear that the Black population obtains a median score about fifteen points below that of the White population. This means that 85 per cent of the Black population scores below the median IQ (100) of the White population; however, it also means that 15 per cent of the Blacks receive higher IQ scores than 50 per cent of the Whites in the United States. In more concrete terms, it is important to realize that there are 3.5 million Blacks who score higher than 83 million American Whites. It is apparent that, in numerical terms, there are substantial degrees of overlap between these two populations. The point here is that both groups, Black and White, have large numbers of individuals, numbering in the millions or tens of millions, above the average IQ range and below it as well.

Nevertheless, how does one account for the average difference in the performance of Black and White populations on IQ tests? Two alternative explanations have been suggested to account for the observed difference. One hypothesis attributes the difference to environmental factors. The other suggests that genetic factors are the sole or major cause of the average differences observed. In view of the sharply differing experiences of Black and White populations in the United States, the environmental hypothesis is clearly a plausible one. Indeed, it is the hypothesis that has been followed by most psychologists, educators, and anthropologists. But not all workers in these fields subscribe to the environmental explanation. They suggest, instead, that the differences in IQ test performance may reflect differences in the gene pool of various racial groups as well as environmental differences. They suggest that the lower average performance of American Blacks may reflect a lower frequency of genes for average or above-average intelligence. The notion of race, they point out, is based on the existence of different frequencies of an unspecified number of genes among different breeding populations. They suggest as a possibility that, just as races differ in the frequencies of the genes for blood type, skin color, and hair form, they could also differ in the frequency of genes that determine intelligence. This could be reflected, they suggest, in the lower average scores of some populations on that imperfect measurement of intelligence, the IQ test.

They fail to point out, however, that if there are genes that contribute to the determination of IQ test performance, they need not necessarily occur in only two forms, good and bad. It would be possible for these genes, if they exist, to occur in several alternative forms, each directing the production of a different, but competent, phenotype. This is true in the case of the various blood types, A, B, O, and so on. Although different, all the genes determining the blood type contribute to the production of competent blood cells. It is not surprising to find that even though races differ in blood-group frequencies, they all make, to the best of our knowledge, equally competent blood. Hence, we find it unnecessary to segregate pints of blood on the basis of race in blood banks. These considerations make it clear that it would be quite possible for races to differ in their frequencies of the genes that determine IQ and yet not differ in the competence of the product of these genes.

In recent years Arthur R. Jensen, a professor of psychology at the University of California at Berkeley, and William Shockley, a Nobel-prize-winning physicist and professor at Stanford University, have, along with some others, strongly argued that heredity is the sole or crucial factor in determining the difference in the average IQ scores of Blacks and Whites. For an examination of their arguments in their fullest subtlety and most forceful presentation, the reader is urged to consult their writings, especially that of Professer Jensen referred to in the bibliography at the end of this book. However, in summary form, their arguments can be stated, I believe fairly, as follows:

1. The strongly heritable nature of IQ makes it likely that an appreciable fraction of the fifteen-point differential in the mean IQ of Black and White populations is genetic.
2. The average distribution of IQ scores in American Blacks is not only lower than that of Whites but also lower than some groups of an even more economically disadvantaged minority, the American Indian. Furthermore, on tests of scholastic achievement and certain subtests of the IQ test, Blacks received lower scores than Whites, Oriental Americans, and some groups of other disadvantaged minorities, such as Mexican Americans, Indian Americans, and Puerto Ricans.
3. When American Black and White children were grouped into five socioeconomic levels ranging from high to low and their average IQs were compared, Black children averaged lower than White children in their own or even lower socioeconomic levels.

Before we consider each of these arguments in turn, it is interesting to note that, even if we accepted all of them uncritically, either individually or collectively, they could not demonstrate that genetics is the crucial factor in bringing about the average difference in the IQs of Black and White populations. This is because the conclusions were not drawn from studies where the only difference between the populations examined was race. This is a consequence of the fact that these populations, the Black and the White, differ not only in race but in numerous aspects of their present and past environments. It is well known that historically and currently the American White and the American Black populations are divided one from the other. By and large, these populations learn in different schools, from different teachers, and with different classmates. They live in different neighborhoods, earn different salaries, and, we are beginning to realize, think different thoughts and honor different values. Because of the sharp separations between Blacks and Whites or even between Blacks and other minority groups, the comparative performance of other disadvantaged minority groups on IQ tests is not necessarily very helpful in interpreting the average difference in Black and White IQ scores. We turn now to a detailed examination of each of the arguments advanced here.

1. *The assertion that IQ is strongly heritable.* Those writers who suggest that the Black-White IQ difference is primarily due to genetic factors accept the proposition that genes are responsible for three fourths or more of the variation in IQ seen between different individuals. As we have seen earlier, this judgment is based primarily on twin and adoption studies. We have already examined some of the difficulties inherent in making a precise determination of heritability from twin studies. And, we should point out that some respected individuals, such as the Harvard group led by Christopher Jencks, have, after examination of much of the same data used by Professors Jensen and Shockley, concluded that the heritability of IQ is much lower than the 80 per cent usually cited by these workers. Writing in *Inequality,* their now classic attempt to identify the factors that lead to stratification in American society, Jencks and his colleagues concluded, after an analysis of the available data, that the heritability of IQ in the White population could be as low as 0.45 and was likely not higher than 0.60. Furthermore, an examination of some of the twin studies reveals that some of the landmark studies in this field, so often cited by Professors Jensen and Shockley, contain inconsistencies or methodological difficulties so serious that close examination of them has caused Professor Kamin to write: "A critical review of the literature produces no evidence which would convince a reasonably prudent man to reject the hypothesis that intelligence test scores have 0 heritability." In *The Science and Politics of IQ,* Kamin details the inconsistencies and methodological sloppiness that characterizes the most famous and often cited twin study, that of the English behavioral geneticist, the late Sir Cyril Burt. He also points out the ambiguities in other similar and often cited studies by Shields; by Newman, Freeman, and Holzinger; and by Juel-Nielsen.

So far our discussion has pointed out the uncertainties about the precise value of the heritability of IQ in White populations.

Earlier we found that the value of heritability for a trait measured in one population cannot be assumed to hold in other racial populations of the same species. As of this writing, little data exists on the heritability of IQ in Black populations. One is placed in the position of guessing the heritability of this trait in Black populations from the imprecise estimates that have been made in White populations. It would be very difficult indeed to say that the variation in average IQ scores between Black and White populations can be charged to heredity because we do not know with precision what proportion of the variation within the White population is genetically determined and because we have no consistent measure of its value in Black populations. So we are left in the position of not really knowing how strongly heritable IQ is in one population and not really knowing whether it is heritable or not in the other.

2. *The assertion that comparative studies of IQ scores in different minority populations demonstrate that average differences between Black and White populations are genetic rather than environmental.* It is certainly true that Puerto Ricans, Mexican Americans, and most certainly American Indians have been the victims of disadvantage and discrimination. These populations share an equal burden of economic disadvantage with Blacks. In the case of the Indians it is probably an even greater burden. Why then do these groups not provide the comparisons necessary to adjust for whatever cultural and economic disadvantages exist between White and Black populations? Ignoring for the moment the fact that none of these groups shares a slave heritage with Blacks, we cannot overlook the profound difference between them and Blacks in school environments. A glance at Table 7-2 demonstrates that other minority groups attended schools with predominantly White student bodies and faculties. Interestingly, some studies show that Blacks enrolled in predominantly White schools, like Indians and other minority groups, scored higher on achievement tests than Blacks in predominantly Black schools. When one recalls the use of predominantly White reference populations in the construction and standardization of IQ tests, the difference in school experience that most Blacks have had and the one that other minorities have had is an environmental factor that can hardly be ignored.

3. *The assertion that comparisons of Black and White children from different socioeconomic levels rule socioeconomic factors out as being responsible for differences in the average IQs obtained by Black and White populations.* Comparisons of Black and White children of apparently similar socioeconomic levels also include environmental variables that often go unrecognized. The living patterns of Whites are much more stratified according to socioeconomic

level than those of Blacks. Given the more homogeneous composition of White neighborhoods and schools, the White child often finds that his associates and schoolmates are from a socioeconomic range similar to his own. This is not as often so with the Black child of higher socioeconomic status. Because of the traditionally restricted pool of housing available to Blacks, the neighborhoods and the schools that serve them tend to be much more socioeconomically mixed. Remembering that the majority of the Black population is at a low socioeconomic level, it can be predicted that Blacks at a higher socioeconomic level, as opposed to Whites, will more often find that their classmates and associates are of lower socioeconomic level. Finally, we need to inquire into the uniformity of socioeconomic level in Black as opposed to White families. Is it not likely that the Black of higher socioeconomic level is the only one in the family to have "made it"? On the other hand, is it not more usual for Whites, even of low socioeconomic level, to be able to point to a relative of high socioeconomic level than it is for Blacks? Clearly,

Table 7-2. *Racial Composition of Schools Attended by Various Groups*

	Nationwide (Percentage of indicated population in schools with indicated characteristics)					
	Mexican American	Puerto Rican	American Indian	Oriental American	American Black	American White
Elementary School						
Mostly White students	59	52	66	63	19	89
All White teachers	75	68	77	74	53	88
Secondary School						
Mostly White students	72	56	72	57	10	91
All White teachers	73	57	75	57	25	89

	Urban South (Percentage of indicated population in schools with indicated characteristics)	
	American Black	American White
Elementary School		
Mostly White students	7	91
All White teachers	49	89
Secondary Schools		
Mostly White students	4	95
All White teachers	3	92

From "Equality of Educational Opportunity," a report to the United States Department of Health, Education and Welfare, by James F. Coleman, et al., 1966.

one does not adequately match the socioeconomic level of Blacks and Whites by merely matching incomes and job titles, as was done in the studies most often cited by Professors Jensen and Shockley. The problem has many more levels than these two surface parameters. In this regard, it is interesting to mention a study of the relationship between race, IQ, and social class published by Paul Nichols and E. V. Anderson in 1973. The study is important for three reasons. First of all, the Black and White populations compared were more carefully matched for socioeconomic status than were the populations cited in previous studies. There was attention paid not merely to family income, but to such factors as whether or not members of the sample populations lived in similar neighborhoods and attended similar schools. Most important of all, the sample populations were matched for pre- and postnatal care. As the data in Table 7-3 show, the sample populations were large and the reliability of the testing procedure—the individually administered Wechsler intelligence scale for children—is high. An examination of the data produced by this study shows that whether one is considering Black and White populations in Boston or Black and White

	Verbal IQ				Performance IQ			
	Boston		Baltimore–Philadelphia		Boston		Baltimore–Philadelphia	
Race	White	Black	White	Black	White	Black	White	Black
Number in sample	4,699	491	530	4,098	4,701	490	530	4,091
Mean IQ	102.9	99.3	93.7	91.1	105.5	101.2	98.5	93.4
Δ	3.6		2.6		4.3		5.1	

	Full-scale IQ			
	Boston		Baltimore–Philadelphia	
Race	White	Black	White	Black
Number in sample	4,721	492	535	4,121
Mean IQ	104.2	100.0	95.3	91.2
Δ	4.2		4.1	

Table 7-3.
Distribution of Wechsler Intelligence Scale for Children's IQs by Race and Locality

From Paul Nichols and E. V. Anderson, "Intellectual Performance, Race, and Socioeconomic Status," *Social Biology,* **20** (1973), p. 367.

populations in the Baltimore–Philadelphia area, the fifteen-point difference in IQ test scores, which has been so important in fueling the race-IQ argument, has now shrunk to between four and six points. It is of interest to note that this four- to six-point difference found by Nichols and Anderson is within the range of IQ differences observed between pairs of identical twins, who are by definition genetically identical. Such a small difference in the mean scores of these two populations, whatever its root cause, would not have fueled the derivative arguments about the educational policies of the 1960's, such as the imbroglio over whether one of the fundamental assumptions of compensatory education should be that intellectual potential is essentially equally distributed among Black and White populations. The data presented in the Nichols and Anderson study deal a crippling blow to the hypothesis that holds that the fifteen-point differential observed in a raw comparison of Black and White populations is substantially genetically determined. It is apparent that the appearance of equally careful studies, with results that are congruent with those of Nichols and Anderson, will go a long way toward making the race-IQ argument moot.

In concluding this survey, we must return to a consideration of the fact that attitude and motivation may be important factors in determining performance on IQ tests. These tests are exercises in which there are a number of tasks to be completed in a limited period of time. Suppose we have two individuals of equal intrinsic mental capacity who take the same IQ test. If one of them considers the test an important exercise and applies himself to it with verve and diligence and the other dawdles along, not putting forth his best efforts, we can confidently predict that the more diligent of the two will score higher. But we also know that the higher score reflects a difference in attitude and motivation rather than a difference in intrinsic intellectual ability. This hypothetical situation for generating IQ differences between individuals of equal intrinsic ability is, of course, relevant to comparisons of average scores amassed by different populations. If we want to be sure we are making valid comparative judgments about the actual intellectual potential of different populations, it is necessary to determine whether the performance on an IQ test or portions of an IQ test is significantly affected by attitude and motivation. If these are found to be important, it will be necessary to arrange test situations where the measured levels of attitude and motivation are the same for the Black and White populations whose average IQ scores are to be compared. It is unfortunate that such a tool for the quantitative measurement of attitude and motivation is at present nonexistent and, hence, not in the armamentarium of behavioral genetics. Burdensome and difficult as such quantitative evaluation of these factors may be, to say nothing of the difficulty of standardizing them between populations, their evaluation and standardization are necessary preconditions that must be met before one can conclusively demonstrate that genetic factors make a significant contribution to the observed difference in the IQs of populations whose life styles and value systems are as different as those of Blacks and Whites.

There is reason to believe that genes play a significant role in setting the range of intellectual potential. It is also apparent that environmental factors are important in the expression and development of full intellectual potential. It is a matter of cumulative record that a significant difference, on the order of fifteen points, exists between the IQ scores of Black and White populations in the United States. But it is also a matter of historical record and contemporary reality that Blacks and Whites inhabit uniquely different cultural worlds in the United States. All of these considerations complicate the task of accounting fully for the observed IQ differences between the two populations. Two clear hypotheses have been drawn: one holds that the difference is totally environmental and the other argues that genetics is the significant factor behind the observed difference. That environment plays a role in producing the fifteen-point spread is granted by even the most able proponents of the hypothesis that favors a significant hereditary generation of diversity. They have suggested that allowance for gross differences in the income and social standing of the races would reduce the difference from fifteen to perhaps eleven points. The advocates of environmental determination feel that if other environmental factors, such as those of culture, history, and motivation discussed earlier, could be adequately evaluated, the interracial difference would be reduced to zero.

It should be clear that conclusive identification of the factors responsible for racial differences in IQ test scores, whether environmental or genetic, will be technically extremely difficult to make. It is apparent that, given present information and methodologies, no decision can be reached as to which of these two positions is correct. However, subscription to one or the other of these presently competing hypotheses has implications that extend beyond science into areas of social concern. Which of these two views is adopted by the larger society and its decision makers will have an important effect on the direction and goals of our public policies. Many who have examined the history of race relations in the United States and around the world feel that of the two alternative hypotheses currently before us, subscription to the genetic one carries considerable potential for mischief. It is for this reason that such emphasis has been placed on exposing the difficulties of the work that must be done before this genetic view can be raised from the level of a

Choosing Between Conflicting Hypotheses

mere hypothesis to the status of a scientifically demonstrated fact.

It is likely that public policies based on the belief that differences in the environment account for the Black-White difference would differ from policies based on the alternative genetic hypothesis. Subscription to the environmental view suggests that improvement of the environment, extension of opportunity, and efforts to compensate for obvious social, educational, and economic disadvantages, if sufficiently massive and continuous, will narrow and eliminate the gap. Such a hypothesis leads to the conclusion that there are few American Black plumbers, executives, and stockbrokers because social factors have operated to exclude them. Subscription to such a view leads to a policy of actively opening up opportunities and, if it is properly applied, to identifying and rigorously training capable people for them. On the other hand, a plausible extension of the genetic hypothesis suggests that the underrepresentation of Blacks in some areas of the society is, as one might expect, because the pool of able individuals is proportionately lower in that population. On the basis of a genetic hypothesis, low achievement scores by whole groups, or throughout an entire school or even school system, may be no cause for concern about the quality of the educational experience: The students are assumed to be inherently less able and, hence, can be expected to do less well. Under such a hypothesis the solution to the problem of low achievement scores can be to expect less.

With these considerations in mind it is not extreme to suggest that whichever hypothesis is correct, a belief in the environmental one is likely to lead to social policies aimed at the expansion of opportunities and the inclusion of racial minorities, whereas subscription to the genetic one could produce a policy of contraction and exclusion.

suggestions for further reading

On Genetics

Agricultural Genetics by James L. Brewbaker. Englewood Cliffs, N.J.: Prentice-Hall, 1964. The serious student will find this a good practical and quantitative introduction to the principles of fitness, selection, and heritability raised in Chapters 6 and 7.

"Caucasian Genes in American Negroes" by T. E. Reed in *Science*, Vol. 165 (1969), p. 762. An exposition of the methods of population genetics interestingly and clearly presented.

The Genetics of Human Populations by L. L. Cavalli-Sforza and Walter Bodmer. San Francisco: Freeman, 1971. A comprehensive and rigorous textbook of human chromosomal and population genetics.

Principles of Human Genetics, 3rd ed., by Curt Stern. San Francisco: Freeman, 1973. A highly readable introduction to human genetics that combines relevance with rigor. A recognized classic in the field.

On Evolution

"Cytochrome C: The Structure and History of an Ancient Protein" by R. E. Dickerson in *Scientific American*, Vol. 226, No. 4 (1972), p. 58. A clear and dramatically illustrated description of the way in which the course of evolution can be traced by an examination of protein structure.

Heredity, Evolution and Society, 2nd ed., by I. M. Lerner and William J. Libby. San Francisco: Freeman, 1976. An excellent, up-to-date synthesis of genetics and human affairs.

"The Human Species," an entire issue of *Scientific American*, September 1960. A group of experts view and interpret the evolution of the human species.

Introduction to Evolution, 2nd ed., by Paul A. Moody. New York: Harper and Row, 1962. An excellent general introduction to the subject of evolution.

Mankind Evolving by Theodosius Dobzhansky. New Haven, Conn.: Yale University Press, 1962. A distinguished scientist and humanist reviews the mechanisms of biological evolution and the significance of cultural evolution.

Mankind in the Making, rev. ed., by William Howells. Garden City, N.Y.: Doubleday and Company, 1967. A highly readable and often chatty view of man's ascent from distant ancestors.

The Naked Ape by Desmond Morris. New York: McGraw-Hill, 1968. A highly readable essay on man that effectively exposes his animal origins and the continuing influence of those origins on human nature.

On Anthropology

Culture and the Evolution of Man edited by M. F. Ashley Montagu. New York: Oxford University Press, 1962. A group of experts tries, often successfully and usually readably, to integrate man's cultural development with his biological evolution.

Culture and Society by Barton M. Schwartz and Robert H. Ewald. New York: Ronald Press, 1968. A good basic introduction to peoples and their cultures.

Invitation to Anthropology by Douglas L. Oliver. New York: Natural History Press (for the American Museum of Natural History), 1964. An economical survey in which the bare bones of anthropology are quickly exposed.

Prehistoric Man, 7th ed., by Robert J. Braidwood. Chicago: Scott, Foresman, 1967. An excellent brief survey of the interface between archaeology and anthropology.

"The Study of Race" by S. L. Washburn in the *American Anthropologist*, Vol. 65 (1963), p. 521. A leading anthropologist acknowledges the existence of human races and puts their formation and shaping in proper cultural perspective.

On Race

"Cyanate and Sickle Cell Disease" by A. Cerami and C. M. Peterson in *Scientific American*, Vol. 232, No. 4 (1975), p. 44. An interesting outline of what may prove to be a successful therapeutic strategy for a serious genetic disease.

From Slavery to Freedom by John Hope Franklin. New York: Alfred A. Knopf, 1956. A complete and thoughtful history of the American Black from his African beginnings to the post-World War II period.

"The Genetics of Human Populations" by L. L. Cavalli-Sforza in *Scientific American*, Vol. 231, No. 3 (1974) p. 80. Hereditary differences and similarities are clearly and authoritatively put in perspective in this article by a leading geneticist.

Human Races by Stanley M. Garn. Springfield, Ill.: Thomas, 1965. A good little book on the external and internal taxonomy of human races.

"Lactase Deficiency: An Example of Dietary Evolution" by R. D. McCracken in *Current Anthropology*, Vol. 12 (1971), p. 479. Together with the articles by Kretchmer and Simoons, a dramatic illustration of the role that can be played by culture in shaping one aspect of a population's genetic structure.

"Lactase and Lactose" by Norman Kretchmer in *Scientific American*, Vol. 227, No. 4 (1972), p. 70.

The Living Races of Man by Carleton S. Coon. New York: Alfred A. Knopf, 1965. For the student who is seriously interested, this book is a relentless, consistently literate, occasionally overinterpreted pursuit of human diversity.

Man's Most Dangerous Myth: The Fallacy of Race by M. F. Ashley Montagu. New York: Macmillan, 1965. A distinguished anthropologist who rejects the concept of race tells why.

Man's Rise to Civilization by Peter Farb. New York: E. P. Dutton, 1968. An account of the history and prehistory of the founders of the New World's first high civilization, the American Indian.

Minority Problems edited by Arnold M. Rose and Caroline B. Rose. New York: Harper and Row, 1965. A wide-ranging survey of the uncertain status and problems of racial and religious minorities in America and across the world.

"Model Estimates of the Number of Gene Pairs Involved in Pigmentation Variability of the Negro-American" by Curt Stern in *Human Heredity*, Vol. 20 (1970), p. 165. Like the article by Harrison and Owen, an interesting exploration of that most visible and possibly least important of racial traits, skin color.

"Primary Adult Lactose Intolerance and the Milk Drinking Habit: II. A Culture-Historical Hypothesis" by F. J. Simoons in *American Journal of Digestive Diseases*, Vol. 14 (1969), p. 819.

"Sickle Cells and Evolution" by Anthony C. Allison in *Scientific American*, Vol. 195, No. 2 (1956), p. 87. A lively exposition of the interaction of an environmental factor, malaria, and a genetic factor, the sickling gene, in the shaping of human populations.

"Skin-Pigment Regulation of Vitamin D Biosynthesis in Man" by W. Farnsworth Loomis in *Science*, Vol. 157 (1967), p. 500. The origins of skin color are considered, and a plausible explanation for differences in the skin color of different racial groups is advanced.

"Studies on the Inheritance of Human Skin Color" by G. A. Harrison and J. J. T. Owen in *Annals of Human Genetics*, Vol. 28 (1964), p. 27.

On Race and Mental Ability

"Biogenetics of Race and Class" by Irving Gottesman in *Social Class, Race, and Psychological Development*, edited by M. Deutsch, I. Katz, and A. R. Jensen. Holt, Rinehart and Winston: New York, 1968. This article represents a clear and economical introduction to the possibilities and limitations of applying behavioral genetics to an examination of racial differences.

Equality of Educational Opportunity (Section 1, a summary). Abstracted from a report by James F. Coleman et al. to the United States Department of Health, Education and Welfare, 1966. Like *Racial Isolation in the Public Schools,* this is a report which has been around for some time now and continues to provide a picture of the comparative character and quality of the public education received by different racial groups in the United States. Such information provides an essential setting for properly viewing comparative differences in the performance of various racial populations on standardized tests.

"How Much Can We Boost IQ and Scholastic Achievement?" by Arthur R. Jensen in *Harvard Education Review,* Vol. 39 (1969), p. 1. After reviewing the evidence establishing that the average performance of American Black populations on IQ tests is lower than that of American Whites, this author suggests that genetic differences in the races play an important role in establishing the observed differences in IQ scores.

Inequality: A Reassessment of the Effect of Family and Schooling in America by Christopher Jencks, Marshall Smith, Henry Acland, Mary Jo Bone, David Cohen, Herbert Gintis, Barbara Hayns, and Stephen Michelson. New York: Basic Books, 1972. A group of Harvard investigators take a hard and quantitative look at the factors, including IQ, that are thought to determine one's place in the many strata of American society. They conclude that most of these factors are overrated.

"Intellectual Performance, Race, and Socioeconomic Status" by Paul Nichols and E. V. Anderson in *Social Biology,* Vol. 20 (1973), p. 367. The first large-scale study of the comparative IQs of Black and White populations in which members of the sample population were rigorously matched for socioeconomic level and pre- and postnatal care.

The Nature of Human Intelligence by J. P. Guilford. New York: McGraw-Hill, 1967. A rigorous, but consistently accessible, exploration of the structure and properties of the human intellect.

Race Differences in Intelligence by John C. Loehlin, Gardner Lindzey, and J. N. Spuhler. San Francisco: Freeman, 1975. An excellent "state of the art" review.

Racial Isolation in the Public Schools. A report of the U.S. Commission on Civil Rights, 1967.

Rehabilitation of Families at Risk for Mental Retardation by R. Heber, H. Garber, S. Harrington, C. Hoffman, and C. Falender. Progress report of the Rehabilitation Research and Training Center in Mental Retardation, The University of Wisconsin, Madison, Wisconsin, 1972. A controlled study which demonstrates that intensive exposure to a stimulating and enriched environment can raise the IQs of Black children more than twenty points.

The Science and Politics of IQ by Leon J. Kamin. Potomac, Maryland: Lawrence Erlbaum Associates, 1974. A distinguished psychologist questions the heritability of IQ.

"When Black Children Grow Up in White Homes" by Sandra Scarr-Salapatek and Richard A. Weinberg in *Psychology Today,* Vol. 9 (1975), p. 80. An interesting article which shows that when Black children are raised in middle-class White homes they score above the national average on IQ tests. Taken together, this study and the report of the Milwaukee project, *Rehabilitation of Families at Risk for Mental Retardation,* cited in this bibliography, constitute the strongest evidence that the causes of the fifteen-point gap between the average scores of Blacks and Whites are largely environmental.

index

Jewish populations, G6PD deficiency in, 111
Jews, 5, 6–7, 11
Johnson, Rafer, 12

K

Kamin, Leon J., 137, 142
Karyotype, 24
Kettlewell, H. B. D., 70
Khorana, H. Gobind, 47
King, Martin Luther, Jr., 43
Konking, 22

L

Lactase, 103
Lactose intolerance, 102–105
Landsteiner, Karl, 58
Lee, Tsung Dao, 32
Lutuli, Albert John, 44

M

McAlester, A. Lee, 71, 77
MacArthur, Robert, 68
McCracken, Robert D., 104
Malaria, 96–101
Mathias, Bob, 12
Mediterranean populations, 6, 37
Meiosis, 27
Melanesians, 49
Melanin, 108
Micronesians, 36, 49
Milk, 102–103
Milk sugar, *see* Lactose intolerance
Miscegenation laws, 7
Mitosis, 26
Model systems, 86
Mongoloids, 3, 31–35
Mutations, 23–24

N

Natural selection, 67
Natural variations, 87
Nazi racism, 3, 6–7
Neanderthal man, 75
Negritos, 49
Negroids, 7, 41–44
Nichols, Paul, 145–46
Nontasters, 56
Northwest European, 6
Nürnberg race laws, 6–7, 8

South American Black, 41
Species, 17
Stern, Curt, 135
Stone-age culture, 78
Structure of intellect model, 122
Sub-Saharan African, 41

T

Tagore, Rabindranath, 47
Tasters, 56
Tay-Sachs disease (TSD), 10, 11
Temperature adaptation, 94
Terman, Lewis, 121
Thalassemia, 96–97, 100–101
Thomonys bottae (pocket gopher), varieties of, 31
Tibetans, 35
Twins, identical, 133–36
   studies of, methodological problems, 136–39

U

Ultraviolet light, and vitamin D, 91
Urine, 3, 57–58

V

Variation, 87
Vitamin D, 9, 90–94
Vonnegut, Kurt, Jr., 3

W

Wechsler Adult Intelligence Scale (WAIS), 125, 126–28
White man, 35

Y

Yang, C. K., 12
Yang, Chen Ning, 33
Yukawa, Hideki, 33

Z

Zulu, 78
Zygote, 26